DISCOVERING YOUR DOG TYPE

A New System for Understanding Yourself and Others, Improving Your Relationships, and Getting What You Want in Life

by Gini Graham Scott, Ph.D.
Author of *Do You Look Like Your Dog?*

DISCOVERING YOUR DOG TYPE

Copyright © 2017 by Gini Graham Scott

All rights reserved. No part of this book may be used or reproduced by any means, graphic, electronic, or mechanical, including photocopying, recording, taping or by any information storage retrieval system without the written permission of the author except in the case of brief quotations embodied in critical articles and reviews.

TABLE OF CONTENTS

PREFACE 5
   The Dog Type System 8
   A Typical Workshop 8
   Making Choices 10
   Understanding One's Choice 12
   Putting It Together 14
INTRODUCTION 17
CHAPTER 1: USING THE DOG TYPE SYSTEM 19
   How the Dog Type System Works 21
   Using the Dog Type System 21
   Learning More about Yourself 22
   Learning More about Others for Better Relationships 24
   To Gain Assistance in Everyday Life 25
   To Just Have Fun 26
   Giving Others Insights about Themselves 26
   Get Ready, Set, Go 27
CHAPTER 2: THE DOG PROFILES 29
DISCOVERING YOUR DOG STAR 31
THE WORKING DOGS 33
   Are You a Siberian Husky, Alaskan Malamute, Samoyed, or Akita? 35
   Are You a Boxer, Bullmastiff, or Mastiff? 37
   Are You a Doberman Pinscher or Rottweiler? 39
   Are You a St. Bernard, Bernese Mountain Dog, or Newfoundland? . 41
   Are You a Great Dane? 43
   Are You a Giant Schnauzer? 45
   Are You a Portuguese Water Dog? 47
THE HERDING DOGS 49
   Are You a Collie, Border Collie, or Shetland Sheepdog (Sheltie)? ... 51
   Are You an Old English Sheepdog, Bearded Collie, or Bouvier des Flandres? 53
   Are You a Pembroke Welsh Corgi? 55
   Are You a German Shepherd or Belgian Malinois? 57
   Are You an Australian Cattle Dog? 59
THE HOUNDS 61
   Are You a Beagle or a Basset Hound? 63
   Are You a Dachshund? 65

Are You a Greyhound or Whippet?... 67
Are You an Afghan Hound, Borzoi, or Saluki? 69
Are You a Bloodhound or Coon Hound? 71
Are You an Irish Wolfhound or Otterhound?..................................... 73
THE SPORTING DOGS.. 75
Are You a Labrador or Chesapeake Bay Retriever? 77
Are You a Cocker Spaniel or a Golden Retriever?............................. 79
Are You an English Springer Spaniel or a Brittany?......................... 81
Are You a Weimeraner or Vizsla? 83
Are You an English or Irish Setter?... 85
Are You a Pointer? 87
THE TERRIERS 89
Are You a Bull Terrier, American Pit Bull, or Staffordshire Bull Terrier? 91
Are You a Cairn, Norfolk, or Scottish Terrier?.................................. 93
Are You an Airedale Terrier?.. 95
Are You a Bedlington Terrier, West Highland White Terrier, or Soft Coated Wheaten Terrier?... 97
Are You a Jack Russell Terrier or Fox Terrier? 99
Are You an Irish Terrier, Kerry Blue Terrier, or Schnauzer? 101
TOY DOGS 103
Are You a Pomeranian, Kings Charles Spaniel, Papillion, Yorkie, or Silky Terrier?... 105
Are You a Chihuahua, Chinese Crested, or Pug?............................. 107
Are You a Miniature Pinscher, Italian Greyhound, or Toy Terrier? 109
Are You a Pekingese, Maltese, LlasaApso, Havanese or Shih Tzu? 111
NON-SPORTING DOGS... 113
Are You a Chow Chow or Chinese Shar-Pei?................................... 115
Are You a Bichon Frisé? 117
Are You a Dalmatian? 119
Are You a Poodle?... 121
Are You a Boston Terrier? 123
Are You a Bulldog?... 125
CHAPTER 3: GAINING INSIGHTS INTO OTHERS 127
How the Dog Profiling System Can Up Your Inner Radar 128
Using Dog Types to Make Good Decisions about People 131
The Type of Information Gained Through Dog Type Techniques... 132
Recognizing Different Personality Types and Behavioral Styles..... 135
Summing Up.. 141

PREFACE

DISCOVERING YOUR DOG TYPE features a unique system for understanding yourself and others, thinking about and improving relationships, and having fun in creative, new ways. It's based on learning about yourself and others by knowing what type of dog you each like most or are most like – and calling on different types of dogs for different types of help – such as Guide Dogs for advice, Power Dogs to gain power, and Rescue Dogs for extra help. While this system can be an amusing and whimsical way to think about yourself and others, it offers psychological insights and practical advice on interpersonal relationships. Plus it provides creative ways to solve problems, make decisions, and deal with everyday situations.

As the first book in the series, *DISCOVERING YOUR DOG TYPE* describes the dog-type system and the dog profiles that reflect the different personality types. The next books provide techniques for applying the system to tap powers of your intuition and visualization to gain insights, advice, power, and other types of help in both your personal life and work.

This Dog Type approach to personality typing has the potential to become a worldwide system, akin to the Myers-Briggs personality types and the DISC personality profile, because of the exploding popularity of dogs. A companion approach is the Cat Type system, which works the same way, except instead of selecting different breeds of dogs as your favorite and least favorite dogs, you choose among different breeds of cats.

The Dog Type system should be highly relatable to millions of dog owners and fans, because there are over 78 million dogs in 44% of US households, and even more dog owners around the world. Significantly, almost all dog owners consider their pet a family member, buy clothes and gifts for their dog, and otherwise closely bond with their pet. In turn, the dogs they choose commonly reflect their own personality traits, and knowing these choices can help people better understand themselves and others.

I was inspired to develop this system as a result of writing and collecting photos for *Do You Look Like Your Dog,* which later became a game, fashion show, short documentary, and TV reality show proposal. As I gathered photo submissions of dog owners with their dogs, I noticed that many people not only looked like their dogs, but shared many personality traits. Many people I met also commented on how they shared traits with their dog or chose their dog because of these similarities. At the same time, I was teaching psychological profiling classes for an investigative careers program, and I compared Pomeranian and Siberian Husky owners for a Cal State, East Bay Anthropology graduate seminar and found dramatic personality differences. While the Pomeranian owners were highly social, warm, and friendly, much like their highly social, affectionate dogs, the Siberian Husky owners were an independent, sometimes feisty, group, just like huskies.

As I continued going to dog shows to collect more photos for the *Do You Look Like Your Dog?* book, I noticed differences between the owners of other breeds. Soon a growing number of people shared their stories about why they preferred certain dogs whether they owned a dog or not. Many spoke of their close identification and kinship with their dog. They characterized their dog as a close companion and friend, and described the fun they had together as best buddies. Eventually I did a short documentary featuring owners and their dogs called *What Kind of Dog Are You?*

These comments also reminded me of a variety of workshops I had participated in over the years involving encounters, hypnosis, shamanism, fantasy, theater games, dance, and play. In some workshops people picked an animal guide to help them go on a journey to gain personal insights. Sometimes they chose and "danced" as an animal to feel closer to it and ask for guidance. In still other programs for singles, people described their favorite animal or said what animal other group members reminded them of to better get to know each other. And in some workshops, more like a party, people pretended to be different animals to release their spirit of play and just have fun.

The final piece of the *What's Your Dog Type?* workshop came together when I began to think about the different personality systems I taught in my classes and about the many different systems popularized on the Internet. There are dozens of such systems, from Myers-Briggs Personality Typing, and the DISC Personality Profile to many quick answer tests for self-understanding through associations, such as "What Flavor Fits You?" and "What's Your Pop Star Style?"

Eventually, all of these ideas led to the *Dog Type?* system, which led to a series of workshops on using dog preferences and dislikes to better understand oneself and others, improve relationships, and organize social mixers using a variety of exercises. Later, I used this same approach to create a system for cat enthusiasts: *What's Your Cat Type?*

As an example of how the system works, at one singles program for about two dozen women and men, everyone eagerly spoke about their experiences with different types of dogs. For example, Betty[1] identified herself as a "Poodle" person, though she previously owned a Cocker Spaniel, explaining that: "When I was younger, I liked Cocker Spaniels because they are so friendly and outgoing, and I was much more active. But after my last Cocker died and a friend gave me a Poodle, I felt it was perfect for me. It was quieter, more self-sufficient, and more of a loner, very much like me."

When another group compared the owners and their dogs, Barbara said Mark, a company manager, seemed like a German Shepherd, since he was strong and controlled, but could explode if threatened, like this dog. "This dog is normally a sweet, lovable, great protector, like Mark. The kids tug on his hair, grab his paws, rub his stomach, and he loves it. But when a stranger approaches, he stiffens up and starts growling, till he's sure everything's okay, which is very much like Mark, too."

---

[1] I have used pseudonyms for the participants at the party.

The Dog Type System

Gradually, as I heard hundreds of people explain their reasons for choosing a breed and describe the traits they shared with their chosen dogs, the "Dog Star" system emerged, based on describing a dog's personality traits along 12 dimensions, much like the 12 houses in astrology. These dimensions include characteristics like: size, leadership, dominance, aggression, speed, location, affection, strength, obedience, intelligence, appearance, and demeanor. As I found in the workshops, while some people make choices consciously, because they like a dog's looks or feel it has similar traits to themselves, others feel drawn to a dog, but don't know why. Yet, in either case, when told the traits usually associated with that dog, most people feel the description accurately portrays themselves or others they know.

A Typical Workshop

Here's an example of the workshops I used to develop the system. Each workshop had a similar format. It began with informal introductions followed by a discussion of the dogs people are drawn to and the characteristics of other people they know with these dogs. Then people shared their insights.

At one program, Andrea,[2] who lived in a small apartment complex, described some neighbors who owned a pit bull, which terrified her and several other tenants. Though she didn't know the dog's owners well and was relieved when they left after several complaints, she noticed that they had the same pugnacious, aloof, unfriendly nature as their dog. As she told her story:

"My upstairs neighbors had this female pit bull, and they called her Igor, which is a male Russian name. This dog gave me the creeps. I

---

[2] I've changed the names of workshop participants to protect their identities.

would come home and see her darting around and growling, though she would pull back and let me pass.

One day, the dog was very ferocious when I came home from the grocery store. She was baring her teeth and snarling, and she looked like she was about to jump on me…Eventually I waited it out, and after about 15 minutes, she finally turned away, ran toward a four foot fence around the house, and sailed over it. It was really freaky.

Thinking back now, I feel like these people were exactly like their dog. They kept to themselves. They were not friendly and very aloof. In fact, their dog helped them keep that wall of distance between themselves and the others in the building."

Jim, a student and sometimes bartender, pointed out that sometimes dogs choose people, because they share certain similarities, which is how a friend got his dog. As Jim explained:

"Jerry was walking down the street when this dog appeared. It followed him home, and he fed it and adopted it. It was a tough little mutt, and Jerry is, too. I'm not sure what it was, maybe a mix of Rottweiler, Lab, and Spaniel. But whatever it was, Jerry really took to it, and they had a lot of similarities. Jerry would spend hours at home working at his computer, and he had a pretty solitary job in IT. But he loved to party, like he was two different people. And the dog was like that. It would go off and you might not see it for days…Then, suddenly, it would be back and ready to follow Jerry around, when Jerry began to go out and be more social."

Making Choices

In the next phase of the program, people chose the dog they most preferred or identified with, their second favorite, and least favorite. To help people choose, I used photos of different dogs, along with a brief description of their major characteristics, personality, and temperament. Participants chose among the most common breeds in the seven major groups of dogs, according to the American Kennel Club – working, herding, sporting, and non-sporting dogs, terriers, hounds, and toys.

After people wrote down their top two favorites and least favorite dog, and their reasons for selecting them, they shared their choices and reasons with the group. Their explanations help to show that they were drawn to qualities they saw in themselves and rejected those qualities they didn't have or didn't want. For example:

> Sarah on choosing a Siberian Husky:
> "A friend gave me this Siberian puppy, and I fell in love with her. She was so cute, and I liked her high energy. As she got older, I loved her free spirit and independence. She really had a will of her own, so it was a challenge to raise her. My mother wondered why I would want a dog that didn't listen to me and would run away if I left the door open, so I had to go looking for her. But I felt this close connection, and now, that's what I would choose first – a Siberian Husky. Plus, I feel the Husky is a lot like me. I feel like I have that same kind of free spirit and independence."

> Alison on choosing a Pomeranian:
> "I own a Pomeranian and that's the dog I would choose first, because they're such affectionate and friendly dogs. They love to be around people, and it's such a great companion. I know some people

might get annoyed because they're often underfoot. But that doesn't bother me. Sandy, my Pom, is so lovable, and she's gorgeous, too, with her long reddish brown coat."

Dan on picking a Pug:
"I got a pug, because they are such great companion dogs. They have a very gentle, friendly disposition, and I like that. They may look very pugnacious, but they aren't at all. They like to curl up on your lap, and when I'm working on my computer, my pug Tipi is right there. Tipi is very loyal and good at following orders, too."

Jack on choosing a Golden Retriever.
"For me, a Golden Retriever's a great dog, because I like to go hiking and camping, and this is a sporting dog that likes the outdoors. Plus, he's a great family dog, since he's good with the kids. He's so good natured. That's why I got this dog in the first place, and I would get it again."

As for what people didn't like, these were often the very qualities that others found endearing. But they didn't like those traits, for the same reasons that others liked them, such as illustrated by these comments:

Frank on why he liked Siberian Huskies the least:
"I know a couple of people who have Siberian Huskies, but they are so hard to control. They're like teenagers in that rebellious age. So why would I like a dog like that? They may be cute, but they are constantly getting into trouble. That's not the kind of dog I like, and that's why my favorite dog would be a Collie. They are very helpful, gentle, and eager to please."

Betty on why she liked Afghan Hounds the least:
> "To me, Afghans are just plain snooty and arrogant. I know a couple who own them, and they are like that. They act like they're better than anyone and hardly give you the time of day, unless they think they can get something from you. So I don't trust them. The people are all superficial veneer, and that's what I think of Afghans, too."

Understanding One's Choice

At the end of the workshop, everyone discussed two key questions: "What are the main characteristics of the dogs you most like or most identify with?" and "How well do you think the characteristics you have listed fit you?" After listing these traits, the participants gave examples of how they expressed these characteristics, such as the following.

Sarah, who chose a Siberian Husky, stressed how much she valued independence:
> "I've always prided myself on being independent and a free thinker. That's why I decided to go into business for myself when I was younger. I wanted only me as my boss, so I found a way to be an educational consultant. I didn't like teaching, because I felt there was too much supervision. But as a consultant, I could set my own schedule, because I was the one making the rules."

Alison, who chose a Pomeranian, emphasized her warm and friendly qualities:
> "I've always been a very warm, friendly person. My husband is the strong silent type, and I think that's what drew us together. When we go to

cocktail parties and receptions, I'm usually the one who's going around meeting people, talking to them, and bringing them over to talk to my husband. He's a great creative artist, but still shy, and he likes it when I'm outgoing and help to make the connections for him."

The participants also talked about how they expressed the characteristics they associated with their dog in different situations. Here are some of their conversations.

Frank, who chose a Bull Terrier, which he considered tenacious and feisty like himself, recalled an incident in which he stood up to his boss.

"I was feeling like I was being ignored, when it came time for promotions. I didn't think my boss fully recognized what I had done, since he was a hands-off kind of guy who liked to delegate. So I decided to stand up to him and tell what I did. I started out by being very diplomatic, telling him how I appreciated working in the group and how much our group had accomplished. Then, I pointed out that he might not have been aware of some of the things I had done, and I explained how they might help the company. And the strategy worked. I got a raise out of that meeting and an additional assignment, though it's possible I could have gotten canned."

June, who chose a Lhasa Apso, a glamour dog known for its long silky coat, recalled when she participated in a beauty pageant.

"It was one of my college highpoints, when I won a beauty contest. It was only a local event, but it made me feel really good and my boyfriend at the time was really impressed. Though I didn't enter any more beauty pageants after that, the experience made me even more conscious of fashion and style. And that's been important to me ever since."

Putting It Together

Finally, each workshop ended with a discussion about how the participants might apply what they learned in daily life. Here are a few comments to illustrate:

Jon, who chose a Greyhound:
"I realize that I've always liked to do things fast. I like quick results, and I make snap judgments in entering relationships or breaking up. But sometimes I've regretted my fast decisions, and sometimes the quick results have been wrong. So I sometimes need to take more time to do things or get more information to decide."

Barbara, who chose a Bullmastiff:
"I realize it's really important for me to be a presence, and I like the feeling of power that comes from people paying attention and listening to me. What would I change? Well, maybe there are times I come on too strongly, and I need to temper myself down a little."

Susan, who chose a Hairless Chinese Crested:
"I've always liked being unique and different. I like trying new things, as well as shaking things up – like stating a controversial opinion to see how people react. I think that's amusing and interesting, very much like the dog I like the most. I realize maybe I need to be a little more diplomatic and tactful. But otherwise, I don't want to change. I like the way I am."

These comments illustrate how people see themselves reflected in the dogs they choose and how they get insights from them which they can apply in their daily life.

The following two chapters reflect the *Dog Type* system that developed from these workshops. The next books in the series will describe how to use the system to better understand yourself and others, improve personal and work relationships, and apply these techniques in everyday life.

INTRODUCTION

WHAT'S YOUR DOG TYPE? draws on insights from a variety of areas – everything from psychology, lifestyles and learning to systems for personality typing from Myers-Briggs to astrology.

You'll learn about yourself and others by knowing what type of dog you each like the most or are most like – and conversely, what dogs you like least. Additionally, as described in additional books in this series, you can call on different types of dogs like guides, friends, or teachers for different types of help. For instance, pick a Guide Dog for advice or a Power Dog to gain power. And for more help, seek out some Rescue Dogs.

Why use dogs? One reason is that dogs have developed a very close affinity with humans due to their long history as human's closest companion. It's a relationship that goes back to the Neolithic Revolution 12,000 years ago, when humans first began to domesticate animals, and may even go back to Paleolithic times, when hunters sometimes used dogs to help with the hunt. Researchers believe the dog in Neolithic times was probably first used to herd other newly domesticated animals and as a guardian and companion.

Then, over the millennia, dogs were developed for multiple purposes in different cultures around the world, resulting in more than 400 recognized breeds – plus hundreds more unrecognized ones, as well as thousands of mixed breeds. Such recent mixes include the trendy Puggle – a mixture of Pug and Beagle, and the Cockapoo, a Cocker Spaniel and Poodle mix. Over the years, some dogs were developed to work hard at a variety of tasks, such as herding sheep and pulling sleds (the herding and working dogs), finding and retrieving game (the sporting dogs), killing vermin (the terriers), and being a close companion or lap dog (the toy dogs).

It's no wonder that the different types of dogs, with their wide range of personality types and temperaments, can tell us much about ourselves. Plus, as long-time close companions, dogs can be a source of emotional support, advice, and increased feelings of personal power. In fact, people have long used connections with all sorts of personal helpers, from inner guides and teachers to the Teddy Bear a child talks to as a receptive companion. Even doctors use personal guides, whether imagined, real, or a fluffy toy animal, to help patients feel better.

This first book introduces you to the different dog types. Then, the other books in this series cover these topics:
- Using the big four dog types to guide the way you communicate with others
- Finding your Inner Dog, Top Dog, and Power Dog for personal and professional development
- Getting advice from your Guide Dog to understand others and improve your relationships
- Applying the Dog Type System in everyday life

Start with this first book to understand the basics of the Dog Type system. Then, learn the different ways you can apply it in future books and select the approaches that work best for you.

So now, get started. What your Dog Type -- what type of dog are you? What type of dog is your boss, cousin, best friend, or neighbor? Start by learning about the Dog Profile System in the next chapters. Then, apply it for self-development, improving relationships, and in other ways.

CHAPTER 1: USING THE DOG TYPE SYSTEM

To learn about yourself and others using the Dog Type system, think about your favorite and least favorite dogs or choose the breeds you most and least identify with. Also, think about others you know in the same way. What are – or do you think are – their favorite and least favorite dogs?

Thinking about these preferences gives you insight into yourself or others, because people are drawn to dogs with corresponding qualities or with qualities they would like to have. Conversely, they are pulled away from dogs with qualities they don't have or don't like.

This identification process is much like learning about yourself by knowing your favorite and least favorite colors, cars, house styles, or other choices. This system uses dogs because there are so many different breeds with different personalities and temperaments, which were bred for many different purposes in different places around the globe, and because of their very long and close association with humans.

The type of dog you choose or most identify with reflects the traits you have or would like to have. And if you know which dog another person chooses — or can sense what type of dog a person is most likely to be — you can better understand them and know how to better relate to them.

You might even consider the system as a kind of "Dogology" personality system, which parallels other systems of learning about oneself and others. For instance, one popular way of learning about people is to ask "What's your sign?" referring to one of the twelve astrological symbols. Or if you're involved with the well-known Myers-Briggs personality system you might ask: "What's your type?" referring to the four dimensions of personality – either you're E or I (extrovert or introvert), S or N (sensor or intuitive), T or F (thinking or feeling) or J or P (judging or perceiving).

Likewise, as a "dogologist" or "dogster" for short, you might ask: "What's your dog type?" to learn more about others. Just asking the question is also a way to break the ice and get others to tell you more about themselves. Once you learn about the different types of dogs and the personality and lifestyle characteristics associated with them, you can give others insights about themselves, too. The process works a little like doing a reading with color, Tarot cards, tea leaves, or Rorschach tests. In effect, you are using your "Dog Sense", like dogs use their sense of smell to pick up information about people. They literally sniff you out.

Here's an example of how it works. While I was in the middle of organizing the dog typing system, a carpet sales rep arrived to help her select carpets for two new rooms she added to her house. After she told the rep about her project, the rep asked her, "What type of dog do you think I am?" As I looked at her for a few moments, seeing a heavy-set, 50-something woman with graying hair, glasses, and a warm, take-charge personality, the image of a Chow Chow came to mind, in part because the woman looked something like a Chow with her broad round face and body shape.

So I told her: "You're a Chow Chow" and described the characteristics associated with the Chow – regal in bearing, a little reserved, very alert, and devoted. The rep smiled broadly and immediately agreed. "Yes. You're right. That's me." She felt she had these same qualities and described how she showed these characteristics in various settings. So the initial dog type insights helped open the doors to a deeper conversation.

Using the dog types is also an easy, comfortable door-opener, because it's a fun and whimsical way of characterizing people. When you ask: "What's your Dog Type?" or someone asks you: "What type of dog am I?" they often ask the question with some amusement, which makes people feel more relaxed and comfortable and therefore, more willing to share information about themselves.

How the Dog Type System Works

The Dog Type System is based on grouping the many different breeds of dogs into 24 to 36 major types based on their personality characteristics. The exact number will vary from country to country, based on the breeds that are most popular there.

The personality characteristics in each group represent a mix of traits divided into four categories:
- individual traits (appearance, demeanor, intelligence)
- social skills (affection, obedience, strength)
- energy (energy level, speed, and indoor or outdoor location)
- power (size, aggression, leadership/dominance)

There are 12 dimensions of personality, which are like 12 spokes on a wheel or the 12 houses in astrology, so they are dubbed "Dog Houses" in the system. Each dog – and by extension each person – can be located along each of these spokes (such as being a very small to a very big dog on the size dimension). After you map the personality traits on each of the 12 dimensions, you come out with a personality profile which looks something like a lopsided star when charted, so these are called "Dog Stars".

While dogs, as well as people, vary in their unique combination of traits, the Dog Star Profile reflects the common characteristics associated with a particular breed or similar breeds.

The write-ups about these major types of dogs (i.e.: Are You a Beagle or Basset Hound?) highlight the major personality traits associated with that group – and by extension, the people who choose that type as their favorite dog or dog they most identify with. Plus each write-up includes a little history about each breed.

Using the Dog Type System

Now that you understand the basics of the system, here's how to use it.

First, keep in mind these two basic principles:
- If a person chooses a particular type of dog – or you think of a person as that type of dog — the person is likely to have these traits or is likely to want to develop them.
- If a person identifies a dog as their least favorite dog or the one they are least like, the person is likely not to have those traits or is likely to want to get rid of them.

You can now apply these basic principles in five major ways:

1) To learn more about yourself and work on personal and professional development along each of the 12 personality dimensions.

2) To learn more about others and use that understanding to better relate for various purposes (i.e.: a better relationship, advancement at work, to better manage a team of people). If the person doesn't tell you this information, imagine what type of dog that person is most like.

3) To gain assistance with whatever you are doing in your everyday life, such as getting help with setting goals, making decisions, solving problems, and resolving conflicts.

4) To have fun, using the different dog types in a variety of playful exercises by yourself or with others

5) To provide others with insights about themselves, such as a guide, facilitator, or counselor.

Here's a brief introduction into how to use the system in each of these areas. You'll find more details on what to do in Part II.

Learning More about Yourself

To learn more about yourself for personal and professional development, think of what kind of dog you like the most or which you think most represents you, whether you own the dog or not. Think of this as your "Top Dog".

If you have carefully chosen the dog you own, this may well be your favorite. Otherwise, go through the dog photos and profiles and notice which dog you are most drawn to, whether you are already familiar with that breed or not.

Once you choose a particular dog, take time to get more acquainted with that dog and any others in that group by doing the following:

- Look at the list of personality characteristics, and reflect on how you share those qualities.
- Consider how well those personality traits fit what you are doing in your work and personal life.
- Think about how you might further develop some of these qualities.

For example, say you are drawn to a Poodle, a dog that carries itself with an air of pride, dignity, self-confidence, and style. If you already have those qualities, that's a sign you are very much in tune with who you are and have chosen a dog that perfectly reflects you. If you don't have these qualities, think of your choice as a signal to develop them, and use the image of this dog in various exercises to help you.

Then, think about the type of dog you like the least. Consider this your "Underdog". If you already have a clear choice, use that. Otherwise, go through the photos and profiles to pick the breed you like least. Then, take some time to reflect on why you don't like this type of dog. Ask yourself:

- What qualities does it have that I don't like?
- Are there any qualities that I share which I would like to get rid of?

For example, say you chose the Pit Bull as the dog you like least, because you don't like its angry looks and scrappy nature. If you have a usually sunny, outgoing disposition, that choice could be a good match with who you are. Otherwise, if this dog is much like you, this choice might be a signal to change, by finding ways to become more relaxed and not get angry so easily, to better get along with your family and the people you work with.

You'll see a variety of techniques for further exploring and developing or getting rid of these qualities in a future book.

Learning More about Others for Better Relationships

To learn more about others through Dog Profiling, ask them one or two questions. If you can't get the answers directly from them, imagine the type of dog they most seem to be like. The questions to ask are:
- What type of dog do you like the most?
- If you were a dog, what type of dog would that be?

Then, think about the traits associated with that kind of dog and consider the ways in which the other person is like that dog. If he or she is receptive, ask some follow-up questions to learn more. For example, ask questions such as:
- Why did you choose that particular dog?
- What qualities about that dog do you like the most?

Then, listen. These questions may open up a conversation in which the person tells you more about himself or herself and even tells you stories.

Next ask:
- What type of dog do you like the least?
- If you were a dog, what type of dog would you least like to be?

Again, if you can, ask some follow-up questions, such as:
- Why do you like that dog the least?
- What qualities about that dog don't you like?

Again, just listen.

You can ask these questions in a variety of circumstances from having a serious conversation with someone to introducing a fun icebreaker at a party to getting to know your seatmate on a plane.

You can also use these questions and the insights gained about others in different situations and social settings. For instance, use these questions to discover how to better work with your co-workers or boss. Use them to help people get to know each other at a social event. Or use them to select a team, motivate team members, or promote team building.

If you can't ask people questions directly, you can gain these insights after learning the different profiles by using your power of visualization. Simply imagine yourself asking these questions of others and notice what kind of dog immediately comes to mind. Then, think about the qualities you associate with that breed to help you better understand and relate to that person.

You'll see techniques for better understanding and relating to others in another book in this series.

To Gain Assistance in Everyday Life

To apply the Dog Type System in everyday life, think of different types of dogs as companions or advisers who can help you in various ways.

For instance, look to your "Guide Dogs" for advice with setting goals, making decisions, solving problems, and resolving conflicts. To get this advice, get relaxed and imagine your guide dog is with you. Next, ask a series of questions, such as: "What should I do about my problem with the neighbors?" "Where should I go on my vacation this year?" or "What should I do to get that promotion at work?" Then, listen to the answers your Guide Dog provides, using a variety of techniques to get that answer. In effect, you are getting your intuition to speak to you, and imagining that the Guide Dog is giving you this wisdom helps you tap into it.

To improve your abilities and skills, gain confidence, or increase your feelings of power, you can call on your "Power Dogs", that you think of as especially strong and powerful.

If you still need more help, you can call in some "Rescue Dogs" or perhaps use some "Search Dogs" to increase your creativity, again visualizing your Rescue Dog or Search Dog giving you advice.

You'll see techniques for applying the Dog Type System in everyday life in another book in this series too.

To Just Have Fun

The Dog Type system also lends itself to just having fun, using the different dog types in a variety of playful exercises. These activities can be a way to meet and get to know others in a comfortable, light-hearted atmosphere, along with gaining insights. So you can both get to know yourself and others and have a blast doing it.

For example, you can create a game in which you put the name of a breed of dog on someone's back, and he or she has to guess what dog this is. Or organize people into groups based on the type of dog they choose, and then they can participate in a series of games, in which they compete with other groups. For instance, a competition might be between big dog enthusiasts and little dog fans. Or have a "Come as Your Favorite Dog Party", where everyone comes dressed up as the dog they like the most. The possibilities are endless.

You'll see some suggestions to get you started in this next book.

Giving Others Insights about Themselves

Finally, you can use the Dog Type system to give others understanding about themselves, much like a counselor might give someone a personality profile test or an astrological or Tarot card reading. Or give the test in a group, as a facilitator.

To share these observations with others, first learn the Dog Type profiles. After that you can read and analyze someone's "Dog Type", much as I did when the carpet store rep asked her: "What kind of dog do you think I am?"

The way to do this analysis most effectively is to know the system like a salesperson knowing the product line he or she is selling. Then, let your intuition take over, so an image of the person's "Dog Type" immediately comes to mind.

Afterward, share this image with that person and describe the personality characteristics associated with that dog and how they fit that personality type.

Next, encourage the person to share his or her reactions to your assessment. You can give your comments in a spirit of fun or you can use your initial comments to initiate a deeper exchange. For example, you can use the information you gained from your conversation to help the other person set goals, make decisions, or work on developing desired personal qualities.

Still another way to use these techniques is to organize a small informal gathering or workshop where you use various techniques and group sharing for personal development, improving relationships, and applying the techniques in everyday life. Once you plan what you are going to do, invite people to share their experiences for an hour or so, as described in subsequent chapters.

Get Ready, Set, Go

Now start learning about the different types of dogs. You might consider the process a little like going to the dog races where the goal is finding out: "What type of dog are you? What type of dogs are the people you know or meet?"

So, get ready, get set, go, and race on to the next chapter.

CHAPTER 2: THE DOG PROFILES

The following 40 Dog Profiles are among the most popular types of dogs in the U.S. They are based on grouping dogs according to their size, breed, personality, and temperament, although the number of profiles varies from country to country, based on the most popular dogs in each country. Each profile includes a picture of the most common dogs in that group and a brief description of their breed's history and personality characteristics.

These profiles have been developed from the 12 trait dimensions on the Dog Star Chart, and they range in the strength of that quality from the inner ring (lowest) to the outer ring (highest).These dimensions are like the 12 spokes of a wheel on an astrological chart which create the four sections called "houses". Similarly, there are 12 Dog Houses on the Dog Star Chart. Each type of dog can be plotted on the chart, using the basic characteristics of that type of dog. You can modify these profiles to reflect your associations with a dog of that type.

To map each profile, assess where a type of dog might fall on each of the 12 dimensions or Dog Houses. Then, trace the dots from each dimension or spoke to draw a profile for that type of dog. While placing a dot on each dimension is subjective, based on individual and common associations for that type of dog, this process will give you an overall profile. You can compare the profiles for different types of dogs by holding these maps side by side.

The 12 Dog Star dimensions or Houses are listed below according to the four major traits they represent, which are like the four divisions used in many systems, such as in the Myers-Briggs personality system (Extroversion-Introversion; Thinking-Feeling; Intuition-Sensing; and Judging-Perceiving), the four quarters in Astrology, the four suits in a deck of cards, and the four directions in many Native American systems. The four dimensions or Dog Houses are Power, Energy, Social Skills, and Individual Traits –

the four key areas to help anyone become a well-rounded successful person.

Power Traits
1. Size: Very Small to Very Large
2. Leadership/Dominance: Follower to Leader
3. Aggression: Very Low to Very High

Energy
4. Energy Level: Laid Back/Relaxed to Active/Intense
5. Speed: Slow to Fast
6. Location: Indoors to Outdoors

Social Skills
7. Affection: Reserved to Affectionate
8. Strength: Tough to Gentle
9. Obedience: Independent/Hard to Train to Cooperative/Team Player

Individual Traits
10. Intelligence: Low to High
11. Appearance: Ugly/Ordinary to Glamorous/Attractive
12. Demeanor: Serious to Playful

You'll see them laid out on the chart on the following page.

DISCOVERING YOUR DOG STAR

To determine your Dog Star, first map the traits on each of the Dog Houses for your chosen type of dog. Then, add in your unique traits that make you and your dog who you each are. Start with the overall pattern for the major type of dog you have chosen and use this as a general guide. You can further modify it to create your personality profile. You can use a different color or different type of line to note any differences. Later, you can use where you and your dog fall on these different spokes as a guide for participating in different exercises – or joining with others who share a similar combination of traits with you.

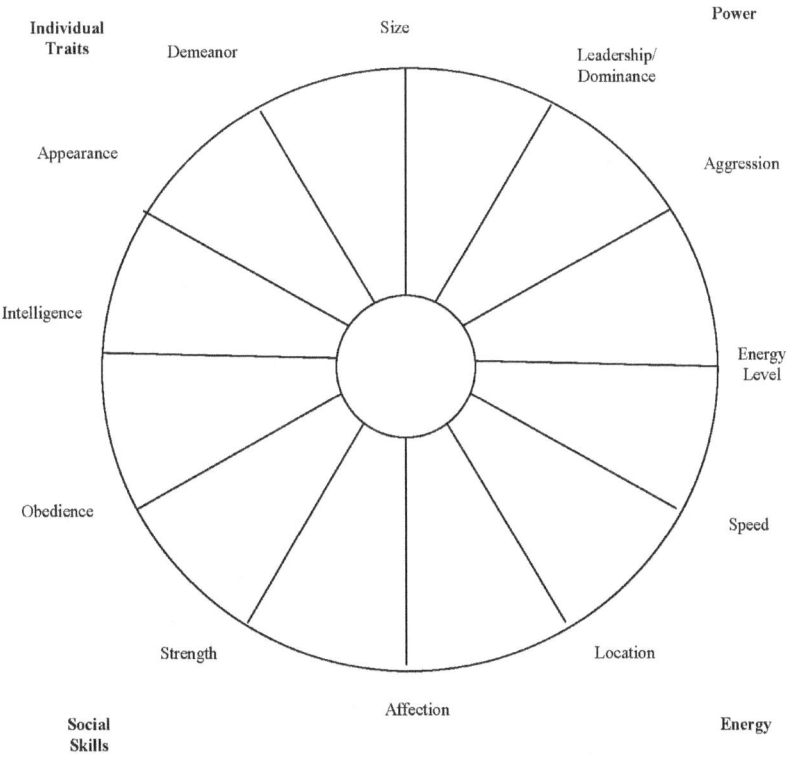

You'll see the Dog Profiles for the major types of dogs commonly known in the United States and Canada on the next 40 pages. Other editions of this book may feature different types of dogs which are relatively popular in these countries.

THE WORKING DOGS

Are You a Siberian Husky, Alaskan Malamute, Samoyed, or Akita?

A Little Bit of History…

In case you chose a Siberian Husky, Alaskan Malamute, Samoyed, or Akita, you have chosen a dog with a close kinship to its wolf ancestors and the Far North.

The Siberian Husky was developed by the Chukchi people of northeast Asia, and was initially used by these nomadic peoples as a sled dog. When the gold rush came to Alaska, these dogs helped the miners carry their gear, and became popular competitors in dog races starting in 1909, when they were first entered in the All-Alaska sweepstakes race. They also gained fame in 1925 when teams of Huskies raced 340 miles from Nenana to bring diphtheria serum to Nome and were honored for saving the town. The current annual Iditarod sled dog race now follows a route from Seward, about 100 miles South of Anchorage, to Nome. Many were recruited in World War II to serve on the U.S. Army's Search and Rescue teams. Now Siberians are a pet as well as a racing sled dog and show dog.

The Alaskan Malamute looks much like the Siberian Husky, except it's larger. They are one of the oldest Arctic sled dogs, and they helped the native Inuit people, known as "Mahlemuts", hunt and haul big game, such as seals and polar bears. When the gold rush arrived, the miners and settlers recruited the Malamutes to participate in weight-pulling contests and races. In the 1920s, they first came to New England, and some gained fame helping Admiral Byrd trek to the South Pole in 1933. They helped during World War II with hauling freight, carrying packs, and search and rescue.

The Samoyeds also originated in ancient times, with the Samoyed people who arrived in northwestern Siberia from Central Asia. These people used their dogs to herd reindeer, protect them from large Arctic predators, and sometimes hunt bears and tow boats and sleds. The Samoyeds first came to England in the late 1800s, and Queen Alexandra helped to promote the breed. In the early 1900s they came to the U.S., and were used on sled teams to Antarctica. They were among the dogs that first reached the South Pole.

The Akita developed in the 1600s in Japan, when a nobleman exiled to the Akita Prefecture, a very rugged, cold area, engaged the landowners in a competition to breed a powerful hunting dog. The result was the Akita, which became renowned for its skill hunting bear, deer, and wild boar. In the 1800s, Akitas were used as fighting dogs, and in 1931, they were honored as one of Japan's national treasures. The first Akitas arrived in America in 1937, and, servicemen also brought them back home after World War II.

What's Your Personality and Style?

If you picked a Siberian Husky, Alaskan Malamute, Samoyed, or Akita, you tend to be **outgoing, friendly, affectionate, playful, fun-loving,** and **adventurous.** You also have a strong **independent, bold,** sometimes **willful, stubborn, tenacious,** and **mischievous** streak, but are still very **loyal** and **devoted** to those you trust and respect, especially family members, and you can be a good **cooperative team player** if you feel so inclined. You are also very aware of **power** in relationships, and either want to be **top dog** or **go along** with whoever is dominant in your group.

Are You a Boxer, Bullmastiff, or Mastiff?

The Boxer dates back to the 1800s in Germany, where it gained early popularity as a contender in the sport of bull baiting. After bull baiting was outlawed, the dog was often used as a butcher's dog to control cattle in the slaughter yards. It also was used by the police and military. Many theories exist about the origin of the breed's name including that the Germans called their butcher's dogs *"boxl"* and because when they fight, they hold their front paws like a boxer. By 1900, the Boxer became a family pet and show dog and since the 1940s its popularity has taken off in the U.S. where it is now one of the most popular breeds.

The Bullmastiff traces its origins to England in the 1800s, where large estates had a problem with game poachers. They needed a strong, tough, courageous dog to quietly wait and attack the poachers without killing them. The result was the Bullmastiff, a cross of a Bulldog and a Mastiff, since Bulldogs were too small and Mastiffs weren't quick enough. They were often called the "Gamekeeper's Night Dog". As the poaching problem declined, Bullmastiffs were recruited as guards and watchdogs, and since the 1920s, have been a show dog and pet.

The Mastiff has ancient roots in England, and when Caesar invaded in 55 B.C., the Mastiffs fought with their masters against the Roman troops. Some of them were brought back to Rome where they were used to fight gladiators, bulls, bears, lions, and tigers. Meanwhile, back in England, they were popular for dog fighting, bull baiting, and bear baiting. Though these activities became illegal in 1835, the fights continued for several decades. Eventually, Mastiffs arrived in the U.S. in the late 1800s, and gradually gained popularity.

What's Your Personality and Style?

If you picked a Boxer, Bullmastiff, or Mastiff, you tend to be outwardly **tough, bold, strong, aggressive, confident,** and **courageous**. Yet, you are **playful, loving, affectionate, docile, gentle,** and **patient** when you want to be. At times, you can be **stubborn** and **hold your ground**, though you are good at **following instructions** when you want. You commonly have a lot of **energy** and **enthusiasm,** and tend to be very **loyal** and **devoted** to those you trust.

Are You a Doberman Pinscher or Rottweiler?

A Little Bit of History…
      If you chose a Doberman Pinscher or Rottweiler, you have picked two of the feistiest fighters.
The Doberman was originally developed in Germany in the late 1890s by Louis Dobermann. As a door-to-door tax collector, he wanted a guard dog to accompany him as he went through unsavory neighborhoods. He crossed a number of breeds to finally get the tough, courageous dog he wanted – a bit of German Shepherd, German Pinscher, Manchester Terrier, Greyhound, and Weimaraner. As the breed spread around Europe and America in the early 1900s, it found a following as a police and guard dog, and later it was recruited to serve in the war effort. Plus it has become popular as a family protector, pet, and show dog.
      The Rottweiler traces its ancestry to ancient times, when it was used to drive cattle and guard the herds. The Roman soldiers took the dogs with them on their campaigns, including one to the town of Rottweil in southern Germany, from which it got its name. Later, when the town became the center of cattle sales, the Rottweiler was a butcher's dog. After cattle driving was outlawed in the mid-1800s and the railroad arrived, the breed nearly disappeared. Then some dog fanciers revived the breed in the early 1900s, and it gained a new appeal as a police dog. Since the 1930s, it has grown in popularity as a show dog as well as a pet, and is now considered the 11th most popular breed in the U.S.

What's Your Personality and Style?

     If you picked a Doberman Pinscher or Rottweiler, you tend to be very **strong, bold, courageous, feisty, self-assured,** and **confident.** You like being **powerful** and **dominant**, and can sometimes be **headstrong, stubborn,** and **domineering.** You are also a **loyal, devoted protector**, and are on the **alert** and **ready to attack**, should you feel threatened. You tend to be **aloof** and **reserved** with those you don't know very well. You are a **hard, dedicated** worker, like being **active,** and enjoy the **outdoors**.

Are You a St. Bernard, Bernese Mountain Dog, or Newfoundland?

A Little Bit of History…

In case you chose a St. Bernard, Bernese Mountain Dog, or Newfoundland, these are working dogs, known for their ability to thrive in the cold.

The St. Bernard dates back to Roman times where they were used in the farms and dairies to guard, herd, and pull equipment. They got their reputation as rescue dogs when they were brought to a hospice in the Alps in the 1600s to be watchdogs and companions for the monks. Their good sense of smell helped them locate travelers lost during storms, and they saved more than 2,000 people. The reputation as rescue dogs and protectors has endured.

The Bernese Mountain Dogs share a similar background in the farms and mountains of Switzerland, where they were originally brought by Roman soldiers. But by the 1980s they almost died out as a breed until a Swiss enthusiast began breeding them again. Now they have acquired a following on farms, at shows, and as household pets.
The Newfoundland was developed in the 1700s on the coast of Newfoundland as a dog that loved the water and could endure very cold weather. It helped the fisherman haul their heavy nets through the water and saved many people from drowning. On land, it was used for hauling and packing.

What's Your Personality and Style?

If you picked a St. Bernard, Bernese Mountain Dog, or Newfoundland, you tend to be **good natured, gentle, affectionate, hard-working, loyal, dedicated, steadfast,** and **reliable.** You are something of a **protector**, wanting to help and protect those you are close to. You also seek out **approval,** like to **please,** are very much a **people dog,** but in a quiet friendly kind of way, where people look on you with trust and respect. You tend to be **down-to-earth** and **serious**, rather than showy and flamboyant.

Are You a Great Dane?

A Little Bit of History...
     Great Danes, as one of the largest dogs, definitely make a statement. In case you chose a Great Dane, here's a little history about them.
     Ironically, the Great Dane didn't develop in Denmark but was probably a mix made by German breeders of the Irish Wolfhound and English Mastiff, about 1,300 years ago. Initially, Great Danes were bred for boar hunting by the Germans to be big because boars were powerful, fast, and savage with large, fearsome tusks. Then, in the 1880s and 1890s, fanciers in Germany, England, and America began to show Great Danes, and they became known as the "king of dogs" or "Apollo of Dogs" for their nobility, courage, speed, and endurance.

What's Your Personality and Style
     If you picked a Great Dane, you like to **stand out** and be **recognized.** You like being **powerful** and **in charge,** yet you are also **gentle**, **easy-going,** and **affectionate** with others, including children. Just think of the **eager-to-please politician**, and rather than only being a member of a team, you like to **shine** through your **star power**. You're also very **loyal** and **dependable,** and are not normally aggressive, unless

stirred to respond, and then you can show great **courage**, since you're not timid. Rather, you're more like the wonderfully **huge friendly father,** who is normally **placid** until threatened, and then you might erupt in anger, but quickly settle down again when the storm is past.

Are You a Giant Schnauzer?

A Little Bit of History...
If you chose a Giant Schnauzer, you have chosen a dog known for being big, outgoing, and playful.

The Giant Schnauzer traces its origins to Germany in the Middle Ages, where it started as a Standard Schnauzer bred big and crossed with a few other breeds to create a powerful dog for driving cattle. Then, for a time these became butcher's and stockyard dogs. In the early 1900s, they were trained as police dogs, and in Germany they continued to be used in that capacity. More recently, they have gained some acceptance as a pet and show dog in the U.S. and other countries.

What's Your Personality and Style?
If you picked a Giant Schnauzer, you tend to be **bold, outgoing, adventurous,** and **playful,** as well as **strong**, **powerful**, and sometimes have a **stubborn, headstrong** streak, yet you are **dependable** and **reliable,** too. You like to be **top dog** and can be **domineering**, but can be willing to **go along** to **get along** with others. You tend to be very **loyal** and **protective** to those you know well, but are more **reserved** with others until you get to know and trust them. You also tend to be very **active** and **outdoorsy.**

Are You a Portuguese Water Dog?

A Little Bit of History...

In case you chose a Portuguese Water Dog, you have chosen a dog known for being affectionate, fun-loving, and that loves the water.

The Portuguese Water Dog's ancestors come from the steppes of central Asia. It was brought to Portugal in the 8th century, where it was used to help fishermen herd fish into nets and send messages from one boat to another or to fishermen on the shore. When the old fishing methods ended, a wealthy shipping magnate, Dr. Vasco Bensuade, promoted the breed in the early 1900s. For a time, the dogs were shown in Portugal and briefly in England in the 1950s, before they began to gain popularity in America, where they were recognized by the AKC in 1984. They have been especially popular as a family dog, and have gotten even more attention after becoming the family pet of the Obamas.

What's Your Personality and Style?

If you picked a Portuguese Water Dog, you tend to be **affectionate, fun-loving,** and have an **easy-going** nature. You are **friendly, adaptable, enjoy being with others,** and make a great companion or **family member.** You also tend to be **adventurous** and **outgoing.**

THE HERDING DOGS

Are You a Collie, Border Collie, or Shetland Sheepdog (Sheltie)?

A Little Bit of History...

If you chose a Collie, Border Collie, or Shetland Sheepdog (Sheltie), these are herding dogs, which are known for their helpfulness, loyalty, and obedience.

Collies date back to the beginnings of history in Scotland and Northern England, when sheepherders first began to use them to herd sheep. Around 1860, Queen Victoria began to sponsor the breed, and they came to the U.S. in the 1870s. They soon gained popularity through literature, such as the stories of Albert Payson Terhune, who celebrated small-town family life in his *Lad: A Dog* books, and in the 1950s the Collie was immortalized on TV as *Lassie*, the ever-loyal farm dog.

The Border Collies similarly trace back to the days of sheepherders, especially in Scotland, and the 18th century Scottish poet Robert Burns celebrated them as a good and faithful dog.

The Shetland Sheepdog, popularly known as the Sheltie, is a miniature working Collie that evolved on the rugged Shetland Islands off the coast of Scotland. They became recognized as a breed in the early 1900s in England and were introduced into the U.S. soon after that.

What's Your Personality and Style?

If you picked a Collie, Border Collie, or Sheltie, you have a great **get-along** personality, as someone who likes being with others. You tend to have a **gentle, mild-mannered** personality, and make a great **follower** and **team player,** because you like to **go along** with what others are doing. You are eager to **please, take directions,** and are good at **following orders.** You tend to be a **very affectionate, loyal,** and **devoted** toward those you know and trust, though you may be more **reserved** with those you don't know very well.

Are You an Old English Sheepdog, Bearded Collie, or Bouvier des Flandres?

A Little Bit of History…
If you chose an Old English Sheepdog, Bearded Collie, or Bouvier des Flandres, these are all very hairy, lovable dogs, best known for herding sheep.

The Old English Sheepdog was developed 150 years ago in the English countryside, where it was mainly used to drive sheep and cattle to the city markets. Sheepdogs were developed with a long coat to insulate them against the cold, damp English climate.

The Bearded Collie gained their popularity in Scotland in the 1500s to late 1700s, where they were used to drive sheep and cattle. In the 1950s, they spread to England as show dogs, and arrived in the U.S. in the late 1960s.

The Bouvier des Flandres developed in the 1600s and was used for herding cattle in the farmlands of Flanders and in northern France. In fact, "bouvier" means cowherder or oxherder in French.

What's Your Personality and Style?
If you picked an Old English Sheepdog, Bearded Collie, or Bouvier des Flandres, you tend to be a **light-hearted, fun-loving, affectionate** person who loves **being with people.** You tend to be **high-spirited, playful**, and sometimes even **rambunctious.** You are also very **loyal, faithful**, and **protective** of those you like and trust. You're very **down-to-earth**, not at all arrogant, and don't care much for style or show.

Are You a Pembroke Welsh Corgi?

A Little Bit of History…
If you chose a Pembroke Welsh Corgi, you've chosen a dog known for its long body, short legs, and perky disposition.

The Corgis got their start in 12th century Wales, where they were used for herding cattle. Their style was to nip at the cows' heels and then duck quickly under their hooves. They were also used to herd sheep and Welsh ponies. Despite their very different breeding as herding dogs compared to the hunting Dachshund, they have much the same look and personality. They, too, since the 1960s, have become very popular pets, especially in Britain, where they were favorites of King George VI and Queen Elizabeth II.

What's Your Personality and Style?
If you picked a Pembroke Welsh Corgi, you tend to be **clever, energetic, perky, bold,** and **courageous.** At the same time, you are **loyal, devoted,** and **very affectionate** and **friendly**; a real **people person.** You like to **please** others and make a great **companion.** You have a great sense of **playfulness** and **fun.**

Are You a German Shepherd or Belgian Malinois?

A Little Bit of History...
If you chose a German Shepherd or Belgian Malinois, you've picked a dog known for its strength and courage, as well as being a popular police dog.

The German Shepherd was developed in Germany in the 1800s to herd and guard sheep. In 1899, the Verein fur Deutsche Scharferhunde SV was formed to improve the breed, so it not only made a great herding dog, but could be very courageous, athletic, and intelligent, making it an ideal police dog. It became a war sentry during WWI. For a time, its name was changed, so it wouldn't be associated with its roots in Germany, but in 1931, its original name was restored. It also gained movie fame as Rin Tin Tin from the silent movie first released in 1922 and then produced as a series of films and TV series, including a 1947 film with child actor Robert Blake and the 1950s TV series *The Adventures of Rin Tin Tin,* thought different dogs were used over the years. It has since been a popular police dog, and has helped in search and rescue operations and detecting explosives, as well as being a popular pet.

The Belgian Malinois developed in Belgium in the 1800s and was also used to herd stock. They became popular in the U.S. after 1911 until World War II and then declined in popularity, though in recent decades have become renowned as police dogs around the world.

What's Your Personality and Style?

If you picked a German Shepherd or Belgian Malinois, you tend to have **lots of energy**, and are very **alert, intelligent,** and **serious.** You can be **stand-offish** when you first meet someone, and tend to be **strong,** and even **domineering**. You are very **protective** of those you are close to, and are very **devoted** and **faithful**. You also have a strong sense of **mission** or **purpose.**

Are You an Australian Cattle Dog?

A Little Bit of History…
    If you chose an Australian Cattle Dog, you've chosen a dog known for its ruggedness and endurance.
    The Australian Cattle Dog was developed in the 1800s in Australia, when cattle were introduced to the newly opened lands for grazing stock. But the cattle became so wild that the traditional herding breeds didn't have the strength or stamina to deal with them. As a result, through the 1800s, breeders worked to develop a new breed by crossing a variety of breeds including Bull Terriers, Dalmatians, Kelpies, and Dingos. The goal was to create a dog that didn't bark and combined herding instincts with endurance, ruggedness, and protectiveness. The Australian Cattle Dog was recognized in 1897, though it took some time to gain popularity in America, and was finally recognized by the AKC in 1980. It has become a pet and show dog, as well as a herder.

What's Your Personality and Style?
    If you picked an Australian Cattle Dog, you tend to be **full of energy, strong,** and **tenacious** as well as **feisty, independent** and sometimes **stubborn.**

THE HOUNDS

Are You a Beagle or a Basset Hound?

A Bit of History...
    If you chose a Beagle or Basset Hound, here's a little history about them.
    The beginnings of the Beagle are lost in ancient history, though the Beagle was one of the small hounds bred for hunting – especially fox hunting in England. Beagles came to the U.S. in the mid-1850s as a popular hunting dog. While some people still use them for hunting individually or in packs, they have become warm, gentle, trustworthy pets.
    The Basset Hound originally came from France several centuries ago and thrived in Europe, especially in France and Belgium, where they were used for trailing rabbits, deer, and other small game. When the Basset Hound came to the U.S. in the 1800s, hunters mostly used them to hunt rabbits and some birds. Like Beagles, they can hunt in packs and alone, and have a friendly, warm personality.

What's Your Personality and Style?
    If you picked a Beagle or Bassett Hound, you tend to be **friendly** with a **gentle, easy-to-get along with** temperament, just like these dogs. You are normally **loyal** and **devoted** to others. You tend to be a fairly **low-maintenance** person, not overly concerned about beauty and grooming, just as these dogs don't require much coat care or trimming. You tend to be **relaxed, laid-back**, and like **lounging around.** Yet you love being **sociable** around people and love to be loved. Your style is **casual** and **informal,** especially if you chose the Basset Hound.

Are You a Dachshund?

A Little Bit of History…
If you chose a Dachshund, you've chosen a dog known for its long body, short legs, and perky disposition.

The Dachshund dates back to the 1500s in Germany, where it was originally used to flush out badgers. In fact, its name means: "badger hound". The dachshund would chase the badger to its burrow, dig into it, pull it out, and quickly kill it. While the original Dachshund had smooth coats, they were bred in two sizes – standard and miniature – and three coats – smooth, longhaired, and wirehaired for different types of hunting, including chasing foxes and other small mammals. Now they have come into their own as a popular family pet.

What's Your Personality and Style?
If you picked a Dachshund, you tend to be **clever, energetic, perky, bold,** and **courageous.** At the same time, you are **loyal, devoted,** and **very affectionate** and **friendly**; a real **people person.** You like to **please** others and make a great **companion.** You have a great sense of **playfulness** and **fun,** too.

Are You a Greyhound or Whippet?

A Little Bit of History...
    If you chose a Greyhound or a Whippet, here's a little history about them. Both are hunting dogs that are best known for being fast – whether on the hunt or in a race.
    The Greyhound has a long history, back to the pyramids of Egypt, where it was a dog of the pharaohs. After further development in the ancient Greek and Roman empires, the Greyhound became popular in England for hunting all types of small game, especially the hare. They were not uncommon in colonial America, too. Greyhounds became track racing dogs in the 1920s, and their popularity races on today.
    The Whippet is a miniature English Greyhound, developed in England about 100 years ago. They were used by the gentry to chase rabbits in a sport that became known as "snap-dog coursing", since the winner was the dog who snapped up – that is caught – the most rabbits. Whippets are still used for racing on a straight course, while their handlers wave towels or rags to encourage them on.

What's Your Personality and Style?
    If you picked a Greyhound or Whippet, you like to do things **fast.** You are **quick-moving,** with lots of **energy** and **enthusiasm**. You can be very **intense** and **focused**, when doing something that's important to you, as you **race** to accomplish whatever it is. You also tend to have a very **friendly, gentle** disposition, are **warm** and **affectionate** and like to **please.**

Are You an Afghan Hound, Borzoi, or Saluki?

A Little Bit of History…

If you chose an Afghan Hound, Borzoi, or Saluki, these are all hunting dogs with a touch of class, royalty, and elegance.

The Afghan dates back to pre-Christian times, possibly to Egypt, and they were raised by the kings of Afghanistan for hunting. In the late 1800s, British officers who had fought in the Indian-Afghanistan wars brought Afghans back to England, and they came to the U.S. in the 1920s and '30s.

The Borzois gained their aristocratic heritage in Russia, where they were bred by the Russian aristocrats for many centuries. They were raised on large country estates where hundreds of serfs helped breed and train them. Even some Mongol Rulers, including Genghis Khan in the 13th century, raised these dogs for hunting. The wolf was the typical target of the chase. In the late 1800s and the turn of the 20th century, they came to England and America.

The Saluki's noble heritage dates back to the beginnings of ancient Egypt around 6000-5000 B.C. before the dynasties of pharaohs and possibly even to the Sumerian empire from around 7000-6000 B.C. They are possibly the oldest known domesticated breed of dog. In fact, their noble status was so great, that the Moslem considered the Saluki to be sacred. They arrived in England in about 1840 and came to the U.S. in the early 1900s.

What's Your Personality and Style?

If you picked an Afghan, Borzoi, or Saluki, you tend to have an **aristocratic** demeanor. You tend to be **aloof, dignified,** and **reserved,** yet reveal a **sunny, cheerful** disposition when you are with others you are close to. You also show great **loyalty, affection,** and a willingness to **please** those you feel worthy of your commitment and trust. Generally, you are **calm** and **even-tempered.** You might think of yourself as the **benevolent ruler**, eager to help your trusted subjects.

Are You a Bloodhound or Coon Hound?

A Little Bit of History...
If you chose a Bloodhound or a Coonhound, here's a little history about them. Both are best known for trailing a scent – whether helping an English detective or a good old boy in the South.

The Bloodhound dates back thousands of years to the earliest scent hounds, and showed up in Europe by the 8th century. William the Conqueror brought them to England in 1066, and many Church officials and monks used them to help in the hunt. They became famed in England and America for trailing suspects, and are frequently used now by Search and Rescue clubs.

The Coonhound developed in the U.S., probably from crossing the Bloodhound and Foxhound in the 1700s. They became most well-known in the southern U.S., most notably in the Appalachians, Ozark, Blue Ridge, and Smoky Mountains, where they were used to trail raccoons, opossums, and bears.

What's Your Personality and Style?
If you picked a Bloodhound or Coonhound, you tend to have a **relaxed, laidback, calm** nature, though you enjoy being **active** and **playful** at times. You tend to have a strong **independent** and **stubborn** streak, so you may enjoy **going off on your own** and really **sticking to things** you like to do. Yet, while you are generally **warm** and **gentle** with those you consider friends and family, you are more **reserved** or **shy** with strangers.

Are You an Irish Wolfhound or Otterhound?

A Little Bit of History...
      If you chose an Irish Wolfhound or Otterhound, you've chosen a big gentle hunting dog with lots of hair.

The Irish Wolfhound dates back to ancient times in Ireland, possibly brought by the Greeks in 1500 B.C. They were acclaimed for their ability to fight wild animals and were used by the Irish chieftains to hunt wolves, elk, and other game. Ironically, they nearly died out in Ireland after the wolf went extinct, because so many were given to foreign nobles. But they were revived in the late 1800s and have gained increasing popularity for their easygoing, gentle nature that has led them to be dubbed "the gentle giant".

      The Otterhound dates back to the 13th century and maybe earlier in England, where they were used for hunting – especially for finding otters that were preying on fish in the local streams and rivers: hence its name. It became especially popular as a hunting dog from the middle to the end of the 19th century in England, and the first Otterhounds arrived in the U.S. around 1900. But while one of the most ancient of breeds, it is relatively unknown today.

What's Your Personality and Style?

If you picked a Wolfhound or Otterhound, you tend to have a **gentle, mellow** nature, though you like to be **active** and love the **outdoors**. You are generally **calm, sensitive, patient,** and **easygoing**, with a **sweet, loving, affectionate** disposition. Though you may be **reserved** with those you don't know, you are **very warm** with those you know and trust. When necessary, you can show **courage** and **independence**, though you are usually **gracious** and **eager to please.**

THE SPORTING DOGS

Are You a Labrador or Chesapeake Bay Retriever?

A Little Bit of History...

If you chose a Labrador Retriever, including a Black, Chocolate, or Yellow Lab, or a Chesapeake Bay Retriever, you've chosen a dog known for retrieving game that has become a very popular family pet.

Ironically, the Labrador Retrievers didn't originate in Labrador, but in Newfoundland in the early 1800s. There they retrieved not only game but fish, and they pulled small fishing boats through the water by swimming. Though the Labradors died out in Newfoundland because of a steep dog tax, some retrievers were taken to England, where they became known for retrieving upland game. At first they were just black, but soon chocolate and yellow labs were developed, and by the early 1990s, the Labrador had become the most popular breed in the U.S., including being owned by President Clinton, who chose a Chocolate Lab and named him Buddy.

The Chesapeake Bay Retrievers were developed in the U.S. in the 1800s after an English ship went down off the coast of Maryland, and sailors on an American ship rescued their cargo and crew, which included two Newfoundland pups that some rescuers adopted. They turned out to be great water retrievers, and after they were bred with several other dogs, including the Irish Water Spaniel, Newfoundland, and

Bloodhound, they became known for their ability to retrieve ducks in the icy Chesapeake Bay Waters – hence their name.

What's Your Personality and Style?

If you picked a Labrador Retriever or a Chesapeake Bay Retriever, you tend to lead a **well-rounded, active** life. You tend to be a good **people person,** someone who is generally **amiable** and **friendly.** You enjoy **pleasing** others, have an **upbeat, positive outlook,** and tend to be very **devoted, dependable**, and **obedient,** because you want to do what it takes to **get along with others**. You tend to be **gentle, non-aggressive,** and **adaptable,** ready to **conform** and be a **good team player**.

Are You a Cocker Spaniel or a Golden Retriever?

A Little Bit of History...

In case you chose a Cocker Spaniel or a Golden Retriever, these are both sporting dogs which are among the most popular family dogs.

Cocker Spaniels date back to the 1360s in England, where they were divided into land and water spaniels. The cockers were the smallest of the sporting dogs, and they initially helped hunters by flushing out game, generally small birds. They first came to the U.S. in the 1880s and quickly became beloved as a family companion, because of their energetic, friendly, affectionate personality.

The Golden Retrievers were developed in Scotland and England in the early 1800s to help with retrieving game from the water as well as on land, and they came to the U.S. in the 1890s. They are especially known for their obedience, and have become popular as guide dogs for the blind, as well as good at detecting narcotics for the police, because of their sensitive smell ability.

What's Your Personality and Style?

If you picked a Cocker Spaniel or a Golden Retriever, you tend to be a **very affectionate, warm, outgoing, extroverted people-person**, with **lots of energy**, just like these dogs. You are often **playful,** and can be very **charming,** but you're **down-to-earth,** even **humble** in your nature, not showy or ostentatious. You have an **optimistic, cheery** outlook, and are **loyal** and **devoted** to others. No wonder you are likely to be **popular** and enjoy **socializing** with others, just like these dogs.

Are You an English Springer Spaniel or a Brittany?

A Little Bit of History...

If you chose an English Springer Spaniel or a Brittany, you've chosen a dog known for both being game dogs and a family pet, with a sense of class.

The English Springer Spaniel traces its roots to the Cocker Spaniel, and was originally distinguished for its larger size in the early 1900s. Like the Cocker Spaniel, it was popular as a gundog for hunters, and used to both flush and retrieve game. It also boasts a royal heritage, since the Duke of Norfolk in England bred some of the early Springers. Now it has become both a popular show dog and pet, and still retains its sense of royal class. President George W. Bush chose an English Springer Spaniel as one of his dogs.

The Brittany was developed in the mid-800s, when French sportsmen crossed English Setters with their own small land spaniels. Soon the Brittany became popular with the French gentry, who liked their ability to both point and retrieve, combined with an eager desire to please and be obedient. These dogs were also popular with the French artists, and many appear in 17th century paintings and tapestries. They became a recognized breed in the early 1900s. After coming to the U.S. in the 1930s, they grew in popularity as a hunting dog, especially for birds. Plus the Brittany has become a popular city dog, too.

What's Your Personality and Style?

If you picked an English Springer Spaniel or a Brittany, you tend to be **friendly, cheerful, enthusiastic, energetic,** and **eager to please.** You can be very **playful** and **ready for fun,** and you enjoy both being **active outdoors,** as well as **relaxing at home.** You also tend to be good at **following orders, conforming** to what others want, and being **obedient,** though you have a **curious, independent** nature, too. But generally, when asked, you'll give up your independence to **follow the rules.** Plus, you have an air of **dignity** and **elegance.** No wonder people love to have you around.

Are You a Weimeraner or Vizsla?

A Little Bit of History...
     If you chose a Weimeraner or Vizsla, you've chosen a dog with a touch of nobility.

The Weimeraner is a relatively recent breed, developed in the early 19th century, possibly from a line of Bloodhounds, to become one of the hunting breeds in Germany. He became a favorite with the nobles in the court of Weimar, who took him out to hunt game – and hence the name. The nobles particularly liked the Weimeraner's good sense of smell, speed, intelligence, and courage. While he was initially used to hunt big game, he was trained to hunt birds and upland game. Eventually, he arrived in America in 1929, and has since become a popular pet. He has also gotten a reputation as a sensitive artist's model, used to pose in human-like shots by artist William Wegman, and he was portrayed as the neurotic, high-anxiety dog in the movie *Best of Show.*

     The Vizsla's roots date back to the Magyars who came to Europe and settled in Hungary over 1,000 years ago. Hunters used Vizslas to point and retrieve birds and track other game through the woods and underbrush, and by the 18th century, the breed had become a favorite with the barons and warlords of the day. After World War II, as the Hungarians fled from the Russian troops, they took their dogs to other countries, including the U.S.

What's Your Personality and Style?

If you picked a Weimeraner or Vizsla, you tend to combine a lot of **energy** and **enthusiasm,** even a **rambunctious exuberance,** with a **sensitive** and sometimes **stubborn** and **shy nature.** Still, you can be **friendly, courageous,** and willing to **conform** when you want to. Plus you usually have a **gentle**, **affectionate** manner, and you can be particularly **devoted** to those you trust. Additionally, you tend to have a **proud, dignified** manner, as if you have a little **royalty** in your veins.

Are You an English or Irish Setter?

A Little Bit of History...
     If you chose an English or Irish Setter, these are bird and gaming dogs, developed in England and Ireland.

     The English Setters were developed in 14th century England, and trace their ancestry to the Springer Spaniel, Water Spaniel, and Spanish Pointer. They were especially popular as bird dogs and excelled at finding and pointing out game in the countryside. They were first shown in the 1850s and from there spread to the U.S.

     The Irish Setter developed out of the English Setter and possibly the Spanish Pointer and another less well-known setter from Scotland, the Gordon Setter. They are especially known for their mahogany red coat, thought some have white coats. Like the English Setters, they also became popular bird and game dogs.

What's Your Personality and Style?
     If you picked an English or Irish Setter, you tend to be **very active,** enjoy **physical activity,** and are drawn to the **outdoors.** You tend to be very **friendly, amiable, outgoing,** and **easy-going,** a good **people person** who gets along well with others. You tend to be **calm**, with a **mild,** "it doesn't bother me" **disposition.**

Are You a Pointer?

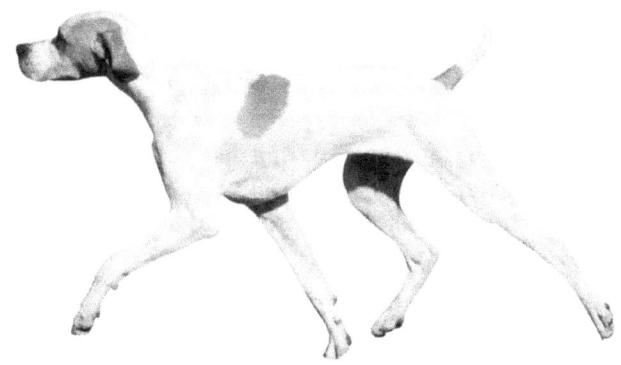

A Little Bit of History…
     If you chose a Pointer, including the German Shorthaired or Wirehaired Pointer, you gained your reputation pointing out hares. The first Pointers originated in England in the 1600s, probably from a mix of Greyhounds, Foxhounds, Bloodhounds, and Spaniels. Their primary job was to point out hares, and once they did, Greyhounds were sent out to pursue the prey. In the 18th century, when wing-shooting became popular, the Pointers were called on to locate birds. They gained their name and fame because on finding the game, the dog would indicate its location by remaining still and pointing at it, while the hunter got ready to shoot.

     The German Shorthaired Pointers go back to Germany in the 1600s, with a mix of English Pointer and a few other strains, including a bit of hound. They were especially well known for not only pointing but retrieving, trailing, and even killing game. They were recognized as a show breed in Germany in the late 1800s and arrived in the U.S. in 1920.

     The German Wirehaired Pointer was developed in the 1800s as a general hunter from the Shorthaired Pointer mixed with some other breeds, including the Polish Water Dog, which contributed the more furry look. They were bred for their versatility in not only pointing, tracking, and retrieving game, but also acting as a companion and watchdog. The rough wiry coat was developed to help the dog get through thick brambles when hunting. They gained their recognition in the show world in the 1920s, and came to the U.S. then, too.

What's Your Personality and Style?

If you picked a Pointer, including the German Shorthaired or Wirehaired Pointer, you tend to lead an **active** lifestyle, enjoy **physical exercise**, and like the **outdoors.** You also tend to be very **focused, direct,** and **to-the-point** in your style; you might consider yourself a real **straight-shooter** and have a sense of **serious dignity** about you. You're a **good, hard worker,** too, with your intense **concentration** and **focus** – your **nose to the grindstone**, so to speak. You are also especially **loyal** to friends and family and like to **please,** though you may tend to be **aloof** and **reserved** with strangers.

THE TERRIERS

Are You a Bull Terrier, American Pit Bull, or Staffordshire Bull Terrier?

A Little Bit of History...

In case you chose a Bull Terrier, American Pit Bull Terrier, or Staffordshire Bull Terrier, you chose a dog originally raised for dog fighting, yet very lovable and affectionate. They all include a mix of Terrier and Bulldog.

The Bull Terrier dates back to the 1800s in England where it was originally developed as a fighting dog for bull-baiting. When dog fighting was outlawed in the mid-1800s, some owners turned to showing their dogs, and when one owner, James Hinks, crossed the Bull and Terrier with a White English Terrier and a Dalmatian in 1860, the first white Bull Terrier was born. Gradually, with some more breeding, the Bull Terrier gained its longer head and some color, too. Most recently, the Bull Terrier has gained fame as a film and advertising personality, such as in ads for Target stores.

The American Pit Bull was brought to America in the late 1800s, where it became bigger than its English cousin and was the most popular dog fighter. Yet, while a fighter in the pits, the dog was bred to be docile and obedient, too, to respond to its owners. Recently, though, the Pit Bull has gotten a bad reputation from being used for illegal fighting and being involved in vicious attacks in the inner cities, though it is popular among other pet owners as a fun-loving, sweet-natured dog.

The Staffordshire Bull Terrier was also developed in England in the 1800s, where it was popular for dog fighting, but friendly toward people when not fighting. After dog fighting was banned in England, it became mainly a show dog, though some enthusiasts still fight their dogs in secret gatherings.

What's Your Personality and Style?

If you picked a Bull Terrier, Pit Bull, or Staffordshire Bull Terrier, you can be an **aggressive fighter** when provoked, in a competitive situation, or when being **protective** of others. But at other times, you can be very **docile, sweet-tempered, loving, affectionate**, and **devoted** to those you are close to. You also tend to be **stubborn, tenacious, strong-willed, courageous**, and **assertive.** You commonly have lots of **energy,** like **action,** and may be even somewhat **exuberant** and **rambunctious.** If you picked a Bull Terrier, you tend to have a **comical, mischievous** side, as well.

Are You a Cairn, Norfolk, or Scottish Terrier?

A Little Bit of History...
    If you chose a Cairn, Norfolk, or Scottish Terrier, you chose one of the classic terrier types, known for their fearless and feisty character.

    The Cairn Terrier dates back to the Middle Ages in Scotland, where it was developed on the Island of Skye, originally for hunting badgers, otters, and foxes. It is closely related to the Dandie Dimont and Skye Terrier, but was eventually distinguished as a separate breed in the early 1900s. It gained fame in the 1940s as the dog that played Toto in *The Wizard of OZ, which was released in 1939.*

The Norfolk Terrier was developed in the 1800s in England. It was originally used for going after rats and foxes, and then gradually developed as a separate breeds in the early 1900s.

    The Scottish Terrier was developed in the 1800s in Scotland, originally for hunting vermin, and is closely related to the Skye Terrier. By the 1880s, it was distinguished as a separate breed and came to America. It grew in popularity in the U.S. after World War II, and one Scottie, Fala, became especially well known as Franklin Roosevelt's constant companion.

What's Your Personality and Style?
    If you picked a Cairn, Norfolk, or Scottish Terrier, you tend to be **bold, feisty, spirited,** and **strong-willed,** have an **independent** nature, and can be **stubborn** and even **scrappy.** You also tend to be very

inquisitive and **curious,** and are eager for **adventure** and **excitement.** You can become very **devoted** and **loyal** to family members and try to **please** those you care about, but you tend to be more **reserved** and show your **independence of spirit** with others.

Are You an Airedale Terrier?

A Little Bit of History...
In case you chose an Airedale Terrier, you have picked a dog known for being big, outgoing, and playful.

The Airedale is the largest terrier, sometimes called the King of Terriers. They originated in the 1800s in England, where they were originally bred to hunt badgers, otters, fox, and other small game. It arrived in the U.S. in the early 1900s, where it continued to be used in hunting, even for big game, and was tapped to work with the police as well.

What's Your Personality and Style?
If you picked an Airedale Terrier, you tend to be **bold, outgoing, adventurous,** and **playful,** as well as **strong, powerful,** and sometimes have a **stubborn, headstrong** streak, yet you tend to be **dependable** and **reliable,** too. You like to be **top dog** and can be **domineering**, but can be willing to **go along** to **get along** with others. You tend to be very **loyal** and **protective** to those you know well, but are more **reserved** with others until you get to know and trust them. You also tend to be very **active** and **outdoorsy.**

Are You a Bedlington Terrier, West Highland White Terrier, or Soft Coated Wheaten Terrier?

A Little Bit of History…

If you chose a Bedlington Terrier, West Highland White Terrier, or Soft Coated Wheaten Terrier, you chose dogs known for being gentle and loving.

The Bedlington Terrier, which looks a little like a lamb, was developed in the 1800s in England and got its name from the mining shire where it was developed. Originally it was used for killing rats, badgers, otters, fox, rabbits, and other small animals. In the late 1800s, the elite in England took a fancy to it, and it became both a show dog and pet.

The West Highland White Terrier goes back about 300 years, where they developed in Scotland to chase down fox, badgers, and other vermin. They were first recognized as a breed by the AKC in 1908.

The Soft Coated Wheaten Terrier got its start in the 1700s in Ireland, initially to help with various farm chores, including rounding up stock and guarding the home. It was late in becoming a show dog, since it only gained recognition in the late 1930s in Ireland and in the mid 1940s in England and the U.S.

What's Your Personality and Style?

If you picked a Bedlington Terrier, West Highland White Terrier, or Soft Coated Wheaten Terrier, you tend to be very **affectionate, gentle, friendly, warm, easy to get along with, playful,** and **fun-loving.** You tend to have a **sunny, happy** disposition. You also are generally **loyal** and **obedient**, willing to **do what's asked**, and enjoy

taking it easy and **being pampered.** Normally, you are **not aggressive** and tend to **avoid confrontations**, but will finally snap back if provoked enough.

Are You a Jack Russell Terrier or Fox Terrier?

A Little Bit of History…
In case you chose a Jack Russell Terrier or a Smooth or Wire Fox Terrier, you chose a live-wire dog primed for excitement and adventure.

The Jack Russell Terrier hails from England in the 1800s, where it was originally used for fox hunting. The breed was initially bred by a Parson named John Russell from Devonshire, England, who loved fox-hunting and wanted a fast-moving terrier that could keep up with the horses and bolt the foxes out of their dens. This Terrier first came to the U.S. in the 1930s, and in the 1990s, they became a popular breed featured in the media as a kind of lovable scamp, resulting in their growing popularity as a pet.

The Smooth Fox Terrier dates back to England in the 1700s, where they were first used to hunt down vermin and find and bolt foxes. They were the first of the Fox Terriers to become show dogs, and for a time, they were crossed with the Wire Fox Terrier, but by the late 1900s, the crossing stopped, and the two types of terriers were classified as separate breeds in 1985.

The Wire Fox Terrier was developed in England in the 1800s, and like the Smooth Fox Terrier, was used for hunting vermin and bolting foxes. It became a show dog about 15 to 20 years after the Smooth variety, and was identified as a separate breed in 1985, too.

What's Your Personality and Style?

If you picked a Jack Russell Terrier or a Smooth or Wire Fox Terrier, you are a real **live-wire**, who loves **action** and **adventure** and has lots of **energy**. You are very **playful, bold, outgoing, friendly,** and **affectionate,** though you may be **reserved** with those you don't know. You also tend to be **inquisitive** and **curious,** and have an **independent, feisty,** and **mischievous** streak that sometimes gets you into trouble. At times, you can be **scrappy**, too. No wonder you are sometimes considered a **lovable rascal** or something of a **clown** and a **scamp.**

Are You an Irish Terrier, Kerry Blue Terrier, or Schnauzer?

A Little Bit of History…
If you chose an Irish Terrier, Kerry Blue Terrier, or Schnauzer, you chose one of the long-legged, fun-loving terriers.

The Irish Terrier originated in Ireland in the 1700s, where it was originally used for hunting foxes, otters, and other small game. It may have a bit of Irish Wolfhound mixed in. It is the fastest of the terriers, with the longest legs and longest body. It became very popular in England in the 1870s and 1880s, and then spread to America. During World War I it was drafted as a messenger and guard dog, but has declined in popularity today.

The Kerry Blue Terrier also originated in Ireland in the 1700s, and was used for hunting rats, as well as foxes, badgers, and even birds. But it was late coming to the show scene, since it was first shown in the 1920s in England and the U.S. It has also been used in police work and training.

The Schnauzer developed in Germany in the Middle Ages. Though it is now classified as a working dog, it was initially considered a terrier, as is the Miniature Schnauzer. It includes a mix of terrier and was originally bred for catching rats, as well as being a guard dog. During the 12th century, the Schnauzer was used to guard farmers' carts in the marketplace. In the late 1870s, it was first shown in Germany, and it came to America in the 1900s. Schnauzers have been used in police work, too.

What's Your Personality and Style?

If you picked an Irish Terrier, Kerry Blue Terrier, or Schnauzer, you tend to be **brash, bold, eager for action** and **adventure,** and like the **outdoors.** You also have an **independent, strong-willed** nature, are very **inquisitive, playful, lively**, and **fun-loving** and tend to be **assertive,** even **aggressive**, or **reserved** with others, though you are **loyal** and **devoted** to those close to you. You may have a streak of **mischievousness** in you, too.

TOY DOGS

Are You a Pomeranian, Kings Charles Spaniel, Papillion, Yorkie, or Silky Terrier?

A Little Bit of History...
In case you chose a Pomeranian, King Charles Spaniel, Papillion, Yorkshire Terrier (Yorkie), or Silky Terrier, these are all feisty, almost catlike Toy Dogs, that make great companions.

The Pomeranians are descendants of the Nordic sled dogs and at one point they were sheep dogs before they were recognized in their diminutive form in the 1870s as a pet and show dog. It is believed they were miniaturized in Germany, particularly in Pomerania, where they got their name. Their popularity spread after Queen Victoria brought a Pomeranian home from Italy, and they were bred in her royal kennels.

The Papillions gained their fame in the 16th century, where they were known as "dwarf spaniels". Initially, they were raised in Spain, then spread to Italy and to France, where they were raised in the court of Louis XVI and became beloved by the artists of the day who included them in many paintings of nobility. After being shown in French dog shows, they spread to England and America in the early 1900s.

The King Charles Spaniel (officially known as the Cavalier King Charles Spaniel) resulted from breeding small spaniels to small Oriental dogs, and the breed became popular in England in Tudor times as lapdogs and foot warmers, and was a favorite of King Charles II. They became very popular in England in the 1900s and later gained recognition in the U.S.

The Yorkshire Terrier was a much later arrival, coming from the working class area of Yorkshire England in the 1800s, where breeders developed many of the Terrier varieties. Despite the Yorkie's lowly origins, the wealthier fanciers were soon attracted to the breed and began showing them. By 1900, the Yorkies had come to America.

The Yorkies played a role in the development of the Silky Terrier in Australia, where breeders combined Yorkies with the Australian Terrier in the late 1800s. By the early 1900s, voila, this new breed was created and came to the U.S. in the 1950s.

What's Your Personality and Style?

If you picked a Pomeranian, King Charles Spaniel, Papillion, Yorkie, or Silky Terrier, you have picked a small but **feisty** toy dog, that is **very alert, vivacious, joyful,** and brimming with **high-energy.** You're also very much the **extrovert**, a real **people-person,** who loves to be with others, and makes a **warm, loving, affectionate** companion. You're usually **obedient, docile,** and **eager to please** others, and you spread your **love** and **affection** around. You love **looking good** and appreciate **good grooming,** and have a high confidence that comes with **knowing you look good**. In fact, your confidence sometimes gets you in trouble, since you're sometimes ready to challenge the "big dogs", using your **cleverness** to outwit and outplay.

Are You a Chihuahua, Chinese Crested, or Pug?

A Little Bit of History…
    In case you chose a Chihuahua, Chinese Crested, or Pug, these dogs are best known for being playful, affectionate companions.
    The Chihuahua's ancestry dates back to the Toltecs in the 9th century and then to the Aztecs in what is now Mexico. They are steeped in legend, and the Aztecs believed the Chihuahua helped guide the soul through the underworld and fight off evil spirits. When Cortes conquered the Aztecs in the 16th century, the dogs were abandoned for a time and ran wild, until a few were discovered in 1850 in Chihuahua – hence the name. After the popular rumba bandleader Xavier Cugat showed off a Chihuahua, their popularity spread in the U.S. and they have gained some fame in the movies, such as in Beverly Hills Chihuahua and Beverly Hills Chihuahua 2, and in commercials, such as the talking dog in the Taco Bell commercials ("Yo quiero Taco Bell).
    The Chinese Crested dates back to 13th century China, when Chinese seamen used them on the ships to get rid of rats and to trade them with the local merchants. Gradually the breed spread to the rest of Asia, Africa, and even Central and South America, where it might have contributed to the Chihuahua. It arrived in Europe in the 1800s and to America in the early 1900s. Though the Hairless Chinese Crested is best known, there is a Powderpuff breed that is covered by a puff of long hair.
    The Pug initially developed in China around 400 B.C. and became a pet for the monks in Buddhist monasteries. From there it spread to Japan and Europe, where it became a popular pet in the royal courts. It even became the official dog of the House of Orange in Holland in the 16th century, after one pug saved the life of William of

Orange by barking at the arrival of the Spaniards. It arrived in England in 1860, after the British raided the Imperial Palace in Peking, and soon after spread to the U.S.

What's Your Personality and Style?

If you picked a Chihuahua, Chinese Crested, or Pug, you picked a dog that is characterized by **playfulness** and **charm**. You are **outgoing, loving,** and make a great **companion,** since you're **devoted** and **eager to please.** You also enjoy **standing out**, **being unique**, the **center of attention**, and the **life of the party.** You have **lots of energy**, too.

Are You a Miniature Pinscher, Italian Greyhound, or Toy Terrier?

A Little Bit of History…

In case you chose a Miniature Pinscher, Italian Greyhound, or a Toy Terrier (either the Toy Manchester Terrier or Toy Fox Terrier), these are small, lively, sometimes scrappy dogs.

The Miniature Pinscher, sometimes called "king of the toys" or Min Pin is a scaled down version of the large German Pinschers, with a mix of Dachshund and Italian Greyhound. The name "pinscher" means terrier. They were developed in the 1600s in Germany and were used to chase down rats in the stables. They gradually spread around Europe in the late 1800s and arrived in America in the early 1900s.

The Italian Greyhounds have a long, ancient history, dating back to the tombs of the Egyptian pharaohs, and they are thought to be the first dogs that were bred to be strictly companions. By the Middle Ages, they had spread throughout Southern Europe, and were especially popular with the Italians in the 16th century, which is how they came to be known as "Italian Greyhounds". Then, they continued to be favorites of powerful nobles and rulers throughout Europe.

The Toy Manchester Terrier (also called the English Toy Terrier) comes from England, where it was first developed in the 16th century, possibly with a little input from the Italian Greyhound. It was especially valued for its ability to kill rates, and it even became a contender in contests to see which dog could kill the most rats in a given time period. Later, it became popular with Queen Victoria.

The Toy Fox Terrier (also called the American Toy Terrier) is a later development by American breeders, who created a new breed from a mix of Fox Terrier, English Toy Terrier, and a little bit of Chihuahua.

What's Your Personality and Style?

If you picked a Miniature Pinscher, Italian Greyhound or English or American Toy Terrier, you tend to be **lively, playful, feisty, energetic,** and sometimes **scrappy.** You tend to be **confident** and **self-assured,** even **bold and brash.** You generally are very **loyal** and **devoted** to family members and those you choose as friends, yet more **reserved** with others, until you develop trust in them. You also have an **inquisitive, curious** nature, and can be **stubborn** and **independent.**

Are You a Pekingese, Maltese, LlasaApso, Havanese or Shih Tzu?

A Little Bit of History...
    If you chose a Pekingese, Maltese, Havanese, or Shih Tzu, you have chosen a Toy Dog, known for its companionship and noble lineage.
    The Pekingese comes from the royal courts of China, dating back to the Tang Dynasty of the 8th century, where they were considered sacred dogs. They were bred and kept in the sacred Buddhist temples and would enter the temples before the emperor to announce his arrival. Should someone steal a sacred Pekingese and be caught, death by torture was the punishment. They arrived in England in 1860 after the British looted the Imperial Palace, and from there spread to the U.S. as a regal lapdog.
    The Maltese's aristocratic heritage dates back to ancient Greek and Roman times, when the dogs were bred on the island of Malta, which was an early trading port. In the 14th century, they were brought to England, where they charmed the upper-class ladies, and by the late 1800s, they spread to the U.S.
    The Lhasa Apso comes from the villages and monasteries of Tibet, where it was believed the souls of the lamas entered their bodies upon death. It first came to England in the 1930s, and has been assigned to AKC's Non-Sporting group, though it looks much like a toy.
    The Havanese are one of the rarer breeds, whose heritage traces back to the Mediterranean and Spain. The Spanish traders brought some Havanese to Cuba where they gave them as gifts to wealthy Cuban women. There they became both pets of the wealthy and performing circus dogs, and after almost becoming extinct, some Cuban families brought them to the U.S. in the 1950s.
    The Shih Tzu, sometimes called the "Chrysanthemum Dog", was developed in China, where they were especially popular with the Chinese emperors. They were bred in the royal courts by the court eunuchs, who

competed to produce the dogs the emperors would like the most. They were frequently pictured in art as hangings or tapestries, and the Buddhists called them "Lion" dogs, which is what the word "shih tzu" means.

What's Your Personality and Style?

If you picked a Pekingese, Maltese, Lhasa Apso, Havanese, or Shih Tzu, you tend to have an **outgoing, friendly, affectionate, happy,** and **trusting** personality. You like the **companionship** of others, and have a **gentle, warm** nature, but combined with a sense of **regal bearing, dignity** and **self-assurance** that befits your royal heritage. You also tend to balance being **playful** and **active** with being very **relaxed** and **laid back.**

NON-SPORTING DOGS

Are You a Chow Chow or Chinese Shar-Pei?

A Little Bit of History...

In case you chose a Chow Chow or Chinese Shar-Pei, these are non-sporting dogs developed in China.

The Chow Chow dates back at least to the Han Dynasty in 150 B.C. when it was developed as a hunting dog. For centuries, the rulers made him their main sporting dog, and one of the T'ang emperors in the 7th century had more than 2,500 of these dogs and 10,000 hunters in his retinue. The dogs were imported from China to England in the late 1700s. Queen Victoria's interest in these dogs helped to increase their popularity in the late 1800s and they came to America in the early 1900s. Since the 1980s, they have become very popular – the 6th most popular U.S. breed according to some accounts.

The Chinese Shar-Pei's heritage dates back to southern China, where it was first raised in a small village, Tai Li in the Kwantung Province, around the time of the Han Dynasty in 200 B.C. Its name: "shar-pei" refers to its rough, short, sandpaper-like coat. Unlike the royal Chow Chow, these dogs were used by peasant farmers as guard dogs, wild boar hunters, and dog fighters. Most of them were eliminated from China when the Communists took over in the early 1920s, but a few were bred in British Hong Kong and Taiwan. Then, in the 1960s, a few Shar-Peis arrived in America, and the breed took off in 1973, when an article referred to them as the "world's rarest dog".

What's Your Personality and Style?

If you picked a Chow Chow or Chinese Shar-Pei, you tend to be somewhat **reserved, aloof**, and **serious,** with a **quiet self-assured dignity.** You might even characterize yourself as **regal** or **lordly** in your bearing. You also tend to be **independent,** sometimes **stubborn,** and while you may show **reserve** to those you don't know, you tend to be very **devoted** and **protective** to family members and those you care about.

Are You a Bichon Frisé?

A Little Bit of History...

In case you chose a Bichon Frisé, these dogs were developed in the Mediterranean in ancient times when a large water dog called the Barbet was crossed with a small white lapdog. One of the dogs in this family, called the Tenerife, developed in the Canary Islands, probably taken there by Spanish sailors. In the 14th century, Italian sailors brought a few of these back to Italy, where they became popular as pets with the upper classes. After the French invaded in the 1500s, the dogs were taken to France, where they became popular with the French kings, Francis I and Henry III. Then, for a time the breed declined in popularity and became a common street dog. However, peddlers and organ grinders found the dogs were good at performing tricks and featured them on the streets and fairs. The breed nearly disappeared during World War I and again due to World War II, but some French breeders helped to keep the breed going, and it came to the U.S. in the 1950s. Finally in the 1960s it gained a new popularity after its hair was cut with the distinctive look it wears today.

What's Your Personality and Style?

If you picked a Bichon Frisé, you tend to be somewhat **fun-loving** and **playful.** You are **lively, high-spirited, bouncy,** and very **friendly** and **outgoing.** You also are **warm, sensitive, affectionate,** and **attuned to others.** And you are usually **happy, carefree,** and have an **optimistic** attitude toward life generally.

Are You a Dalmatian?

A Little Bit of History...
     If you chose a Dalmatian, these are non-sporting dogs that got their name from a region in western Yugoslavia called Dalmatia, though they date back to even earlier times, since their images have been found on Greek friezes and tablets dated back to 2000 B.C. They played many roles, including being a war dog, shepherd, draft dog, ratter, retriever, bird dog, and circus dog. However, in Victorian England, the Dalmatian gained its fame as a coach dog, which both protected the horses from other dogs and looked stylish as they paced before or alongside the coach. They were adopted by fire departments in the 1800s because they were good with horses. Then, with the development of the automobile, they dropped out of being a high society dog though they remained as a coach dog on the fire-engines drawn by horses, and eventually became adopted as a fire-dog by modern fire engine companies. Its distinctive colors helped it become a popular pet and show dog, and after being featured in several children's movies, such as *101 Dalmatians*, it has become even more popular today.

What's Your Personality and Style?
     If you picked a Dalmatian, you tend to be **enthusiastic** and **playful,** and full of **energy**. You love to be **active**, like the **outdoors,** and are sometimes **aggressive** or **reserved** with strangers, and may have a **stubborn streak.** However, you are **outgoing** and **friendly** once you know and trust others, and you are very **dedicated, loyal,** and **love to please.**

Are You a Poodle?

A Little Bit of History...

    If you chose a Poodle, these are non-sporting dogs developed in central Asia, though they are most commonly associated with France.

    The ancestors of the poodle had curly coats and helped with herding. From central Asia they spread to France, Russia, Hungary, and other places in Europe in the 1500s. The Poodle got its name from its German version, where it was called a "pudel", due to its ability to splash in the water. It was also used for hunting ducks and herding in France, as well as being a military dog, guide dog, guard dog, and wagon puller for actors and circus performers. Eventually it became a circus dog, and it got its distinctive pulls of hair on its legs and tail as a result of its role as a performer, though some have claimed these clips helped to keep their joints warm when they were in cold water. Then, in 1700s and 1800s, it was adopted by fashionable ladies and gained favor with the French aristocracy, which led to it becoming the national dog of France. By the late 1800s, it was entered in the show ring, and in the 1900s it nearly died out in America. But in the 1930s, it regained its popularity and became one of the most popular U.S. dogs.

What's Your Personality and Style?

If you picked a Poodle, you tend to be **playful, friendly**, **smart,** and a real **people pleaser.** You like to be **sociable** and like **get along with others,** though you might be **reserved** when you first meet people. You are good at **following directions**, and tend to be **very loyal** and **devoted** to one person. You also tend to be **optimistic** and full of **enthusiasm.** You thrive on **getting attention,** and may tend to be **very self-confident, assured,** sometimes even **arrogant,** because you are used to being admired and shown off for your good looks.

Are You a Boston Terrier?

A Little Bit of History…
In case you chose a Boston Terrier, these are non-sporting dogs that developed in the United States. Starting about 1865, they were bred by the coachmen of some wealthy people in Boston from their dogs, resulting in a cross that combined an English Terrier, Bulldog, and French Bulldog with the dog's distinctive markings, making it look a little like a gentleman in a tuxedo. Interestingly, the dogs they were bred from were at one time fighting dogs. By 1893, they were recognized by the AKC, and by the early 1900s, their popularity spread.

What's Your Personality and Style?
If you picked a Boston Terrier, you tend to be somewhat **playful** and **feisty,** though you are comfortable being **formal** and **business-like** with a sense of **elegance** and **self-importance.** You're also **smart, clever,** and a **fast learner**. You can be very **determined** and **persistent**, and sometimes even **stubborn.** You are quite **sensitive** to others, **devoted** and **loyal** to those you are close to, but you can be **reserved** and **aggressive** to others.

Are You a Bulldog?

A Little Bit of History…

If you chose a Bulldog, these are non-sporting dogs developed in England in the 1200s.

The bulldog was originally developed to bait bulls by attacking and grabbing the nose, making the bull angry, mainly for entertainment, though some thought the bull's meat tasted better as a result of the baiting. Some bulldogs were also used to bait bears, and owners highly valued the dog's aggressiveness. However, after 1835, when bull baiting was outlawed, the breed lost it reason for being, and its popularity declined. But some fans decided to rescue it by selectively breeding to keep its unique physical features while selecting against its aggressiveness. The result was that the bulldog became a very friendly, even clownish dog, though with a tough steadfast persona, that led it to become a show dog starting in 1860, and eventually it became the national symbol of England.

What's Your Personality and Style?

If you picked a Bulldog, you tend to be very **friendly, comical, docile,** and **sociable.** You tend to be very **relaxed, mellow,** and **easy-going,** along with a sense of **modesty** and **humility.** You love to **please others**, but you sometimes can get **stubborn**. You also are characterized by **determination, boldness,** and **loyalty.**

CHAPTER 3: GAINING INSIGHTS INTO OTHERS

The Dog Profile System is a great tool for understanding others, and using these insights to have better relationships at work and in your personal life. The result? More enjoyable relationships by understanding others better, and you can up your chances for success.

Say you have trouble getting along with that cranky aunt when she comes to visit, and each visit usually ends in an argument. By gaining advance insights, you can better know what to say and how to act to get along. Additionally, as you'll discover in other books in the Dog Type series, you can call on your Top Dog or a Power Dog to help you control any angry feelings and hold back from saying or doing anything that might trigger a conflict.

Or say you are going on a job interview. The more you know about how your interviewer thinks, the better you can present yourself. You can use the Dog Profile system, along with visualizing alternate scenarios to help you make a better self-presentation.

This system can also help you tune into the veracity and intentions of the person you are dealing with, so in a business deal, you can use your insight to determine if you can trust and effectively work with a prospective associate. Additionally, the Dog Profiling approach can help you better understand customers or clients, so if you are selling a product or pitching a service, you can better sense what message your prospect would most like to hear. Then, you can tailor your presentation accordingly. The advantages are endless.

How the Dog Profiling System Can Up Your Inner Radar

A key reason that the Dog Profiling approach works well is that it makes your inner radar to others more sensitive by giving you visible symbols to enhance vague feelings and impressions. Then, too, this approach provides you with inner advisers, called Guide Dogs, who can help you through self-talk and dialogue to better evaluate someone or decide your best approach to that person or situation. Other dogs that can help include Power Dogs and Top Dogs you can call on to feel more power and confidence.

This Dog Type method builds on the intuitive approach to understanding others which I first wrote about in *Mind Power: Picture Your Way to Success*. Then, it adds in using Dog Profiles, along with Guide Dogs and Power Dogs, so you can gain more insights to better understand and relate to others.

For instance, when you meet someone, notice what type of dog comes to mind to give you an idea of what that person is like. Or if you are making a decision about whether to work with someone, call on one of your Guide Dogs to help you access your inner knowing or gut level feelings of whether you really want to work with this person.

In effect, consider different types of dogs as amplifiers to help you tap into your inner wisdom in working with others. And the more you access this inner knowledge for one purpose, the more you can apply it in other contexts, such as in resolving problems, making decisions, and setting goals.

Here's an example of how it can supplement this inner wisdom. In this case, Debbie, an artist and designer, used her inner knowing to steer clear of several partnerships that could have been a disaster. Previously, she had gotten into several arrangements with business people, who had taken advantage of her lack of business acumen, and she had unwisely trusted their claims about what they could do, until she later realized these people didn't have the skills or contacts they said. One man who promised to set

Debbie up in a design studio was more interested in a romance with her. A financier talked grandiosely about the financing he could arrange to get Debbie's cards and posters on the market. But then he reported that his business partner had been embezzling from the company, so he had to cancel any new business deals. And Debbie had several other aborted business arrangements.

However, once she discovered how to access her inner impressions to get valid insights into people, she was able to steer clear of the business flakes who made empty promises, and she discovered people who were genuine and sincere. While she used simple visualization exercises to tap into these impressions and feelings, she could have used the advice of her Guide Dogs and the Dog Profiling system to make these insights even stronger and clearer.

In one case, Debbie met a promoter who wanted to start a travel club. He said all the right things to entice her, such as telling her she could design all of the club's materials, get an excellent salary, have travel perks, and even get shares of company stock. So Debbie was enthusiastic about doing some preliminary work on speculation, while funds from a stock issue came through.

But just as they ended their conversation, Debbie's inner radar picked up some danger signals, such as a knotted up feeling in her stomach, which the Dog Profiling system could help her interpret by asking one of her inner Guide Dogs for advice. Or she might get a visual image of a dog associated with that knotted up feeling. Then, if she had negative associations with the dog that appeared – say she thought of a Chihuahua as a sneaky, deceptive dog, like some of the workshop participants did in one of my workshops, that would be a clear message that this person probably had those characteristics, too.

In Debbie's case, her inner warning signal led her to tell the man she would have to think about his proposal (though the Dog Type system might lead to a quicker and surer response, given the strong, clear message). Then, when she did some checking, she learned that this so-called successful promoter was operating his business out of his bedroom. He only had promises of backing, and several people who had worked for him before on spec had ended up with nothing.

Similarly, Debbie used her inner powers a few weeks later when an associate introduced her to a man with extensive video and film credits, and invited her to design some dolls for him.. Yet, as he bragged about what he could do, while dropping many names of well-known people, Debbie heard her inner voice repeating the warning: "Beware...Beware. This man isn't what he seems." Here a Dog Profile could supplement this inner warning with an image of the type of dog representing this man, and the traits associated with this dog could provide more insights into what this man was really like. And questions to a Guide Dog could provide further insights into why the man might not be what he seemed to be.

In any case, the message that this man was trouble came through loud and clear, so Debbie diplomatically explained she was busy with other projects; and later her intuitions were confirmed, when others told her the man was difficult to work with, unrealistic in his expectations, unwilling to listen to reasonable suggestions, and ready to blow up if challenged.

Unfortunately, sometimes it's easier to miss or dismiss these early inner rumblings or not know how to understand their meanings. That's where the Dog Type system could be especially valuable, because it helps to amplify and give these vague impressions more meaning. Then, too, if you work with the Profiling System and your Guide Dogs on a regular basis, your first sign of concern, such as a feeling of anxiety or tension in your stomach, can trigger a review of what's wrong. To conduct this review, you might think about the traits of the type of dog you associate with this person. Additionally, you can ask your Guide Dog for advice on how deal with this person based on your associations about the person based on the dog he or she is like. Then, if you don't like that dog or have negative associations with it, that's an even clearer indication that there's a problem in working with that person or you can act accordingly to work around the problem.

Using Dog Types to Make Good Decisions about People

As Debbie's example illustrates, the Dog Type system is ideal for tapping into your inner knowing to make some quick decisions about people when you first meet. You can ask your Guide Dog for a quick assessment, imagine what kind of dog this person might be, or do both. Then, use that information to decide how to better relate to that person and determine what type of relationship you want, if any, with that person.

Say you meet someone briefly to discuss a possible business venture, and the first image which comes to mind is a Golden Retriever, which is a gentle, friendly, warm, sensitive dog, which likes being around people. It might be good to be open and friendly with this type of person and maybe spend more time engaging in small talk. You might even ask that person about his or her family and share a little bit about yours. By contrast, if the image that comes to mind is a German Shepherd, which is a tough, stern, aggressive dog, which is good at being obedient and following the rules, take a more reserved, strict business approach. Be more direct and get to the point; don't try to schmooze; and keep your approach more business-like and formal.

Or say you are interviewing people to rent a room in your house. You can use the insights you gain from imagining what type of dog each person might be, or you can ask your Guide Dog for advice which might help you decide if you want that person to be your roommate. If you are in sales or pitching or promoting anything, the system is ideal for getting a quick read on someone. Then, you use this information to know how to best approach that person to get a positive response to whatever you are pitching or promoting.

Here's how Paul, who markets health and food products through direct-sales, might use these techniques to custom tailor his presentations and increase his chances of closing a deal. While Paul has dozens of products to show people and a list of over twenty benefits his products offer, he can use this system to select a few products and benefits to emphasize, depending on the insights he gets about a person.

He can begin getting these intuitions with his first phone call. As he asks a few preliminary questions to determine if the person would be a good customer, he can form an image of the type of dog this person might be. Then, the personality traits associated with this type of dog would give Paul an intuitive sense of the person's personality and preferred way of perceiving and receiving information.

When he meets the person, Paul can use this preliminary picture to shape his opening remarks. As they talk further, he can continue to refine this image to better know this person.

The result of this approach is that Paul will have a better rapport with his prospects. Why? Because pre-visualizing who the person is based on the type of dog associated with him helps sense what this person is like and type of approach he or she will be most receptive to. Then, Paul can relate to that person from that person's own perspective. As a result, at their first meeting, after a minute or two to build rapport, Paul can emphasize those features of his products and business he thinks will have the most appeal based on his assessment of that person.

The Type of Information Gained Through Dog Type Techniques

These Dog Type techniques provide insights into others, because they enable you to tune into the other person's inner essence or self, much like you might get a gut level feeling about someone and use that to decide whether to trust him or not. Then, you become more sensitive to what these inner feelings or gut sensations are telling you by associating them with an image or symbol, in this case a Dog Profile or advice from your Guide Dog. As you work with these images and associations, you become more in touch with and better able to recognize what your intuitive feelings are telling you, so you can use them to gain more precise information.

The process works like learning a language. As you gain more vocabulary and are better able to combine words into sentences with layers of meaning, you can more clearly express your thoughts and feelings.

Another way to think of this process is that you first see something normally when you look at it with your eyes. Then, you can see a clearer, larger image when you look through a pair of glasses and can see even better when you use a telescope to bring the faraway image closer. Thus, by adding the glasses and telescope, you see what you want to look at more clearly. It's sharper and larger, so you can see much more detail than with the naked eye.

Similarly, when you visualize images for the types of dogs or use a Guide Dog to express your thoughts and feelings, you magnify and clarify them.

Likewise, you can develop your facility to call on these images to better access your inner abilities and insights. Then, whether you get this information through reflection before you meet, when you first meet, or later interact with someone, you have more detailed and more accurate information to go by in assessing this person.

To complement this inner process, work on become more sensitive to people from external cues, too. As you do, you can call on your Guide Dogs to help and support you by providing you with advice. In turn, your invitation to be there serves as a trigger to be more attentive and observant, much like saying a chant can help you get in a more centered, meditative state, so you become more receptive to the information you receive.

Some ways to become more attentive and receptive to external cues are these:
- Train yourself to become more sensitive to ordinary outer cues, such as clothing, gestures, and facial expressions, because you can learn much about a person's character through his or her outward appearances and behaviors. For

instance, a woman who wears a lot of bright colors to work is probably a more outgoing, friendly, dramatic person than someone who wears blues and browns or soft pastels.
- As you look at a person, ask yourself: "What kind of dog most fits how this person looks or what he or she is doing?" Then, keep on observing and don't try to direct the answer you get. Just let the image of a dog come to you or hear a voice in your head telling you the answer. Then, keep looking, and ask yourself: "In what ways does this person have the qualities of the dog I have associated with him or her?"

You can then go even deeper to discover more about a person's character, sense of integrity, perspective, and preferred way of receiving information and communicating with you. Your Guide Dog can help you learn about someone in four ways:

- To get a quick first impression when you meet someone new (i.e.: listen to what your Guide Dogs tell you, or see a dog representing that person suddenly appear);
- To get an advance impression when you set up a meeting with someone in order to have a better first meeting (i.e. review the Dog Profiles to see which type of dog best fits that person in order to adapt how you act before that meeting;
- To gain a more in-depth understanding of a person (i.e.: have an extended conversation with that person in your imagination or discuss who they are with your Guide Dog, so you can communicate better when you meet);
- To reflect on your meeting and decide how to best follow-up (i.e.: review your meeting in your head through a dialogue with your Guide Dog and ask questions like: "What do you think that person thought of my presentation?" and "How can I make a better presentation in the future?" Then listen as your Guide Dog gives advice).

Recognizing Different Personality Types and Behavioral Styles

Using the Dog Type system can give you these insights, because sensing what dog best matches that person makes you more aware of the person's personality type and behavioral style. Then, you can use this information to make any interaction go more smoothly or decide if you want to interact, continue an interaction, or interact more closely with a person.

The different dogs also provide a more nuanced way of understanding other people that can build on other personality systems which divide people up into a small number of major personality types. These other systems provide a good starting point. Then, incorporate the insights you gain from your associations with different dogs to fill in additional details about a person, so you can better communicate and interact with that person if you wish.

You'll see some examples of these broad personality groupings in the Charts, which I adapted from *Mind Power*. In the Personality Types and Personal Characteristics Chart, each personality type is characterized by certain traits, ways of viewing the world, and preferences in relating to others.

In the Ethical Styles Chart, every person, whatever their personality style, has their own approach to making ethical choices and their own way of relating to the world and others.

There are all sorts of ways of categorizing people in different systems. For example, the DISC theory, developed by William Marsten, who researched the emotions of normal people, categorizes people based on their four major drives into four primary types, which is where the DISC term comes from.(And if you think of a person as a certain type of dog, you can fit them into these four categories, as noted).

- (D) high dominance and directness (Mastiff, Great Dane)

- (I) high influence and interest in people (Pomeranian, Golden Retriever)
- (S) high in steadiness and stability (German Shepherd, Pointer)
- (C) high conscientiousness and competence (Collie, Shetland Sheep Dog).

The psychologist Carl Jung divides people into those who are combinations of thinking and feeling or knowing and sensing, while Katherine C. Briggs and Isabel Briggs Myers, developers of the Myers-Briggs system, added two additional dimensions – extroversion-introversion and judging-perceiving. Other groups use other categories and terms. Whatever the system, you can plug different dogs into those categories, so you can then use the principles from that system.

For example, to take the popular Myers-Briggs system, here's how some of the most well-known dogs might fit in. (Since these are subjective associations, what's most important is the associations you make with different dogs, because you will use the system to first sense what type of dog characterizes this other person. Then, you will look at what this association tells you about this person's personality.) Here are my own associations:

- Extroversion (Pomeranian) – Introversion (Afghan Hound)
- Intuitive (Siberian Husky) – Sensing (Blood Hound)
- Thinking (German Shepherd) – Feeling (Pug)
- Judging (Weimaraner) – Perceiving (Chow Chow)

If you combine the way people primarily look at the world (their perceptual style) with the way they are likely to act and respond (their behavior style), you come up with four major categories of people, which can be a good starting point for creating further subcategories of people. You can associate different types of dogs with each category as in the examples below:

- The Take-Charge Personality (German Shepherd, Mastiff, Pit Bull)

- The Analyzer/Explorer (Siberian Husky, Norwegian Elkhound)
- The People Person (Pomeranian, Pug)
- The Conscientious Planner (Collie, Shetland Sheepdog).

The <u>take-charge person</u> tends to have a strongly developed ability to take in information by hearing it; the <u>analyzer/explorer</u> has a well-developed visual sense; the <u>people person</u> tends to experience sensations and respond emotionally or expressively; and the <u>conscientious planner</u> often has a feeling of knowing or certainty about how things are or will be. Many people may be a mixture of different types.

Whatever personality type system or terminology you use, what's most important is recognizing that people have different perceptual and behavioral styles. To most effectively relate to them, you need to be aware of their perspective, as people are most responsive to someone who relates to them in terms of their point of view. Accordingly, when you associate a person with a particular dog, you can use the qualities associated with that dog to help you pick out a person's major personality traits and behavior style.

Then, use this awareness about this person to better understand and relate to him or her. For example, an employer using this awareness can better manage his employees; an employee can make things go more smoothly with her boss; and a salesperson is more likely to have a receptive customer and close a sale. Likewise, you can use this information to make your personal life go more smoothly, such as understanding how to best interact with your partner, mother, cousin, or finicky aunt.

The major characteristics of people with the four different personality types are illustrated in the Personality Types and Personal Characteristics Chart.[3] This chart also indicates how these people prefer to interact with others. As you pick up information

---

[3] Gini Graham Scott, *Mind Power: Picture Your Way to Success in Your Work and Personal Life*, Changemakers Publishing, 2011, p. 109

from the dog you pick for a person and your associations with that dog, you will improve your abilities to interact with that person (or decide not to interact with them) by keeping these characteristics and preferences in mind.

Personality Types and Personal Characteristics

Personality Type	Major Characteristics	Preferred Types of Response
The Take-Charge Personality	Assertive, aggressive, direct, energetic, organized. Interested in broad overviews, trends. A leader type.	Likes someone to be direct, to the point. Likes someone to get behind his or her ideas, plans, and support them.
The Analyzer/Explorer	Cool, calm, detached, independent. Curious, an explorer. Concerned with seeing how things fit together. An evaluator/analyzer type.	Likes someone to be clear, organized, provide a full picture. Likes someone with an analytical mind.
The People Person	Sensitive, emotional, dependent on others. Concerned with details. Very aware of and responsive to people. Concerned with making things go smoothly. Often a follower or helper type.	Likes someone to provide details. Likes someone to be warm, feeling, responsive.
The Conscientious Planner	Very perceptive, quick to know something. Often critical, judgmental, or feels he or she knows it all. Frequently opinionated, righteous. A good sense of what will happen, how things will turn out. A planner, organizer type.	Likes someone to be agreeable, receptive to his or her ideas. Likes someone to be organized, self-assured, and confident.

The major types of ethical styles based on a person's morality and sense of integrity are described on the Ethical Styles Chart.[4] This will help you decide how far you want to trust the person with whom you are interacting, whatever the personality type.

For example, you might think of a person you associate with a Siberian Husky as something of a pragmatist, who thinks, "What's in it for me?" in deciding whether to follow instructions or not. Such a person might also be ready to head out the door if given the opportunity. By contrast, you might think of the Collie a very steadfast, loyal, and trustworthy dog, always ready to patiently wait, so that a person you associate with a Collie similarly has those qualities.

To gain more insights about ethical considerations and how well to trust someone, get relaxed and ask yourself some questions about that person and how to best deal with him or her, by calling on the wisdom of your Guide Dog. Then, listen for the answers as they come to you.

---

[4] Ibid., p. 110.

ETHICAL STYLES

Ethical Style	Major Characteristics	Considerations When Interacting
The Complete Moralist	Completely honest and expects total honesty and integrity from others. May sometimes be very righteous or have a strong religious base for this morality.	Expect to be very honest and straight with this person. Feel confident that you can trust this person completely.
The Situational Moralist	Adapts his or her ethical response to the situation or person. If others in the situation are behaving morally and ethically, he or she will, too.	Be very honest and straight with this person, and he or she will be honest and straight with you. Also, make sure this person is aware you are doing this, for if this person has any reason to distrust you, you may find he or she is no longer being straight with you, but instead is acting like a pragmatic moralist.
The Pragmatic Moralist	Totally amoral. Acts honestly and ethically when it is to his or her advantage to do so. But can engage in dishonest or unethical activities at any moment, if it seems profitable to do so, and there is a low risk of getting caught.	Be wary in any dealings with this individual. As long as he or she thinks there is some personal gain in it, he or she will be straight with you. But if you lose your value, this person will have no qualms about acting unethically toward you.

Summing Up

By keeping these personalities, behavioral, and ethical styles in mind, you can gain insights about others through the dogs you associate with them and the qualities you associate with those dogs and therefore that person. The process looks like this:

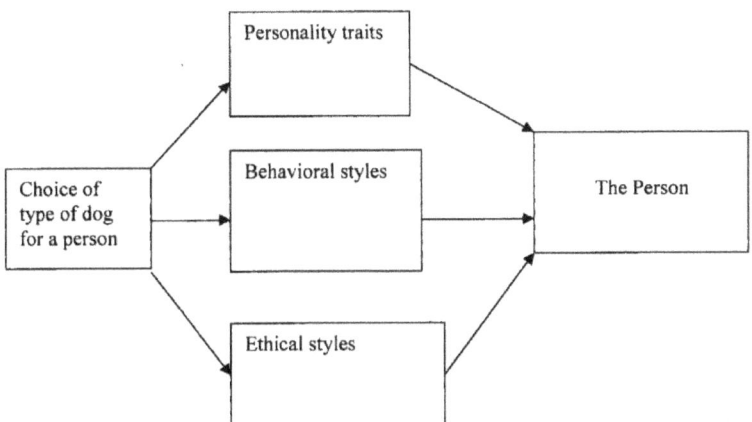

Besides learning about the person and how to better interact based on the dog associated with that person, you can gain further insights by asking your Guide Dogs for guidance. At first, you may need to take time to get relaxed and reflect in a quiet comfortable environment. But as the process becomes more familiar, you can ask a question and get information in response wherever you are.

Other books in this series describe different techniques you can use to get information about others, such as gaining advance impressions before you meet, getting a quick first impression, and gaining more in-depth insights into others. These books also discuss ways to improve your relationships, such as improving your communication, creating a warmer relationship, and increasing your power and influence in a relationship. Plus you can use the 4-Dog Type method to better communicate and work with people in the workplace and in business situations, such as to build teams and more effectively promote and sell your products and services to customers and clients.

SOURCES

The historical material on the different breeds of dogs is drawn from these five books. The information in each book is organized by breed.

AMERICAN KENNEL CLUB. *The Complete Dog Book, 19th Edition Revised.* New York: Howell Book House, 1998.
COILE, D. Caroline. *Encyclopedia of Dog Breeds.* Hauppauge, New York: Barron's Educational Series, 1998.
DEPRISCO, Andrew and Johnson, James B. *The Mini-Atlas of Dog Breeds.* Neptune City, New Jersey: T.F.H. Publications, 1990.
SCHULER, Elizabeth Meriwether. *Simon & Schuster's Guide to Dogs.* New York: Simon & Schuster, 1980.
WILCOX, Donnie and Walkowicz, Chris. *The Atlas of Dog Breeds of the World, 5th Edition.* Neptune City, New Jersey: T.F.H. Publications, 1995.

ABOUT THE AUTHOR

GINI GRAHAM SCOTT, Ph.D., J.D., is a nationally known writer, consultant, speaker, and seminar leader, specializing in social trends, popular culture, business and work relationships, and professional and personal development. She has published over 50 books on diverse subjects with major publishers. She has worked with dozens of clients on memoirs, self-help, and popular business books, as well as film scripts. Her websites include www.changemakerspublishingandwriting.com and www.ginigrahamscott.com. She is a Huffington Post regular columnist, commenting on social trends, new technology, business, and everyday life at www.huffingtonpost.com/gini-graham-scott.

She is the founder of Changemakers Publishing featuring books on social trends, work, business, psychology, and self-help, which has published over 100 Print, e-books, and audiobooks. She has licensed several dozen books for foreign sales, including in the UK, Russia, Korea, Spain, Indonesia, and Japan.

She has written numerous books on creativity and visualization, including *Mind Power: Picture Your Way to Success; The Empowered Mind: How to Harness the Creative Force within You;* and *Want It, See It, Get It!*

She has received national media exposure for her books, including appearances on *Good Morning America, Oprah,* and *CNN*. She has been the producer and host of a talk show series, CHANGEMAKERS, featuring interviews on social trends.

Scott is active in a number of community and business groups, including the Lafayette, Danville, and Pleasant Hill Chambers of Commerce. She is a graduate of the prestigious Leadership in Contra Costa County program and is a member of a BNI group in Walnut Creek, B2B groups in Danville and Walnut Creek, and many other business networking groups. She is the organizer of six Meetup groups in the film and publishing industries with over 6000 members in Los Angeles and the San Francisco Bay Area. She also does workshops and seminars on the topics of her books.

She received her Ph.D. from the University of California, Berkeley, and her J.D. from the University of San Francisco Law School. She has received five MAs at Cal State, East Bay, including most recently an MA in Communications. She will be starting an additional MA program in history there in the fall of 2017.

CHANGEMAKERS PUBLISHING
3527 Mt. Diablo Blvd., #273
Lafayette, CA 94549
changemakers@pacbell.net . (925) 385-0608
www.changemakerspublishingandwriting.com

www.ingramcontent.com/pod-product-compliance
Lightning Source LLC
Chambersburg PA
CBHW070110120526
44588CB00032B/1408